SOME OF THE MEMORABLE LANDMARKS AND LANDFORMS TO BE SEEN IN AUSTRALIA..

SYDNEY
FIRST CITY OF AUSTRALIA

"The city set in jewels" is how the noted Australian writer Henry Lawson referred to Sydney.

As night falls over Australia's first city, a million multi-coloured lights twinkle from windows, blaze from signs, illuminate roadways and sparkle from the waters of Sydney's harbour. The proud span of the Harbour Bridge shines green-gold, while the multiple shells of the Opera House on Bennelong Point rise in glowing curves above dark water. The Sydney Tower at Centrepoint raises a bold golden spear, while reflections from the Darling Harbour complex dazzle in ruby, sapphire and emerald.

"The finest harbour in the world, in which a thousand sail of the line may ride in the most perfect security..." Captain Arthur Phillip wrote of Port Jackson in 1788. Seeking a site for settlement, he had led a small party from Botany Bay northwards to examine the harbour whose entrance Captain James Cook had noted 22 years earlier, but had not explored.

Today, the "finest harbour" is the heart of a magnificent city, where tawny sandstone buildings erected two centuries ago by convict labour stand side-by-side with today's shimmering, tinted, glass-walled towers.

Modern Sydney is multicultural and sophisticated. It looks boldly to the future without forgetting its roots. It is a worthy First City of Australia.

Eastern Rosella on Waratah, floral emblem of New South Wales

LEFT: SYDNEY OPERA HOUSE AND SYDNEY HARBOUR BRIDGE.
INSET LEFT TO RIGHT: A CITY SET IN JEWELS; DARLING HARBOUR; SYDNEY TOWER AT CENTREPOINT RISES ABOVE THE CITY LIGHTS.

ABOVE: THE QUEEN VICTORIA BUILDING, WITH ITS DOMES AND CUPOLAS, WAS ONCE MARKETS AND IS NOW A PICTURESQUE SETTING FOR QUALITY BOUTIQUES.

BELOW: A SPEEDY FERRY CARRIES PASSENGERS BETWEEN CIRCULAR QUAY, THE HISTORIC ROCKS AND THE FANTASTIC DARLING HARBOUR DEVELOPMENT.

ABOVE: NORTH AND SOUTH OF THE HEADS WHICH GUARD PORT JACKSON ARE SUPERB BEACHES. SEEN HERE IS FAMOUS BONDI BEACH.

BELOW: CIRCULAR QUAY, IN SYDNEY COVE, WAS BUILT BY CONVICT LABOUR. THE MOORED SHIP IS A RECONSTRUCTION OF HMS *BOUNTY*.

OPPOSITE: SAILING ON PORT JACKSON.

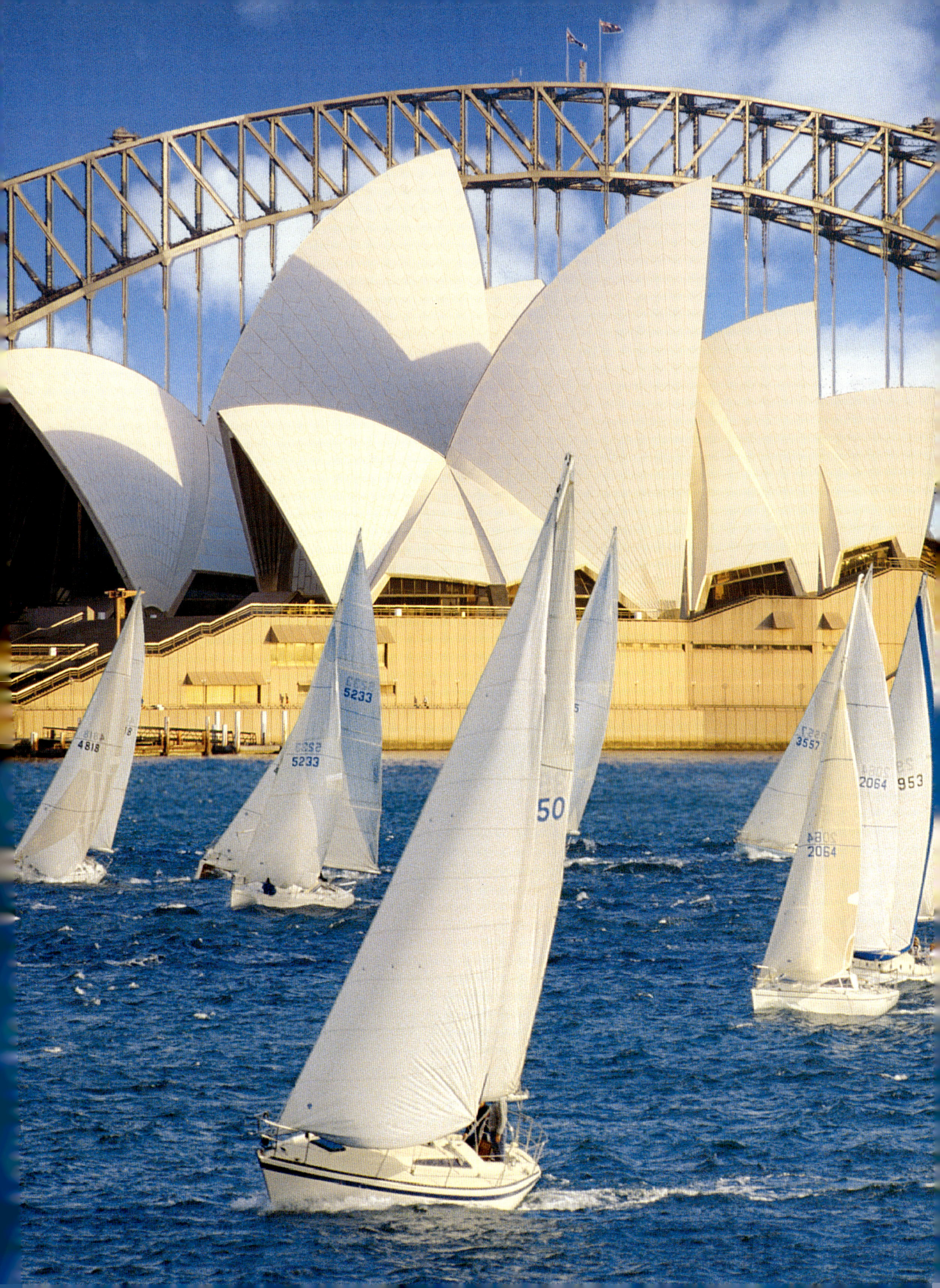
5233
4818
5233
50
3557
2064
953
2064

THE BLUE MOUNTAINS
SPECTACULAR SANDSTONE VISTAS

The Blue Mountains are about 65 kilometres west of Sydney. They are composed of sandstone, deposited up until 170 million years ago, then pushed up into a plateau, disturbed by volcanic activity and finally eroded into deep gorges by weather and rivers. From a distance, the mountains appear hazy blue, an illusion caused by sunlight passing through fine droplets of oil evaporating from the leaves of their abundant eucalypt forests. Spectacular cliffs, fern gullies, waterfalls and wildlife are all parts of the Blue Mountains' scenic attractions and bushwalkers, photographers, birdwatchers and nature-lovers in general find the area particularly rewarding.

ABOVE: SANDSTONE CLIFFS OVERLOOK MIST-FILLED GORGES.
BELOW LEFT TO RIGHT: KATOOMBA; KATOOMBA SCENIC SKYWAY; KATOOMBA ON THE RIM OF JAMISON VALLEY.
OPPOSITE: THE THREE SISTERS, A FAMOUS LANDMARK IN THE BLUE MOUNTAINS.

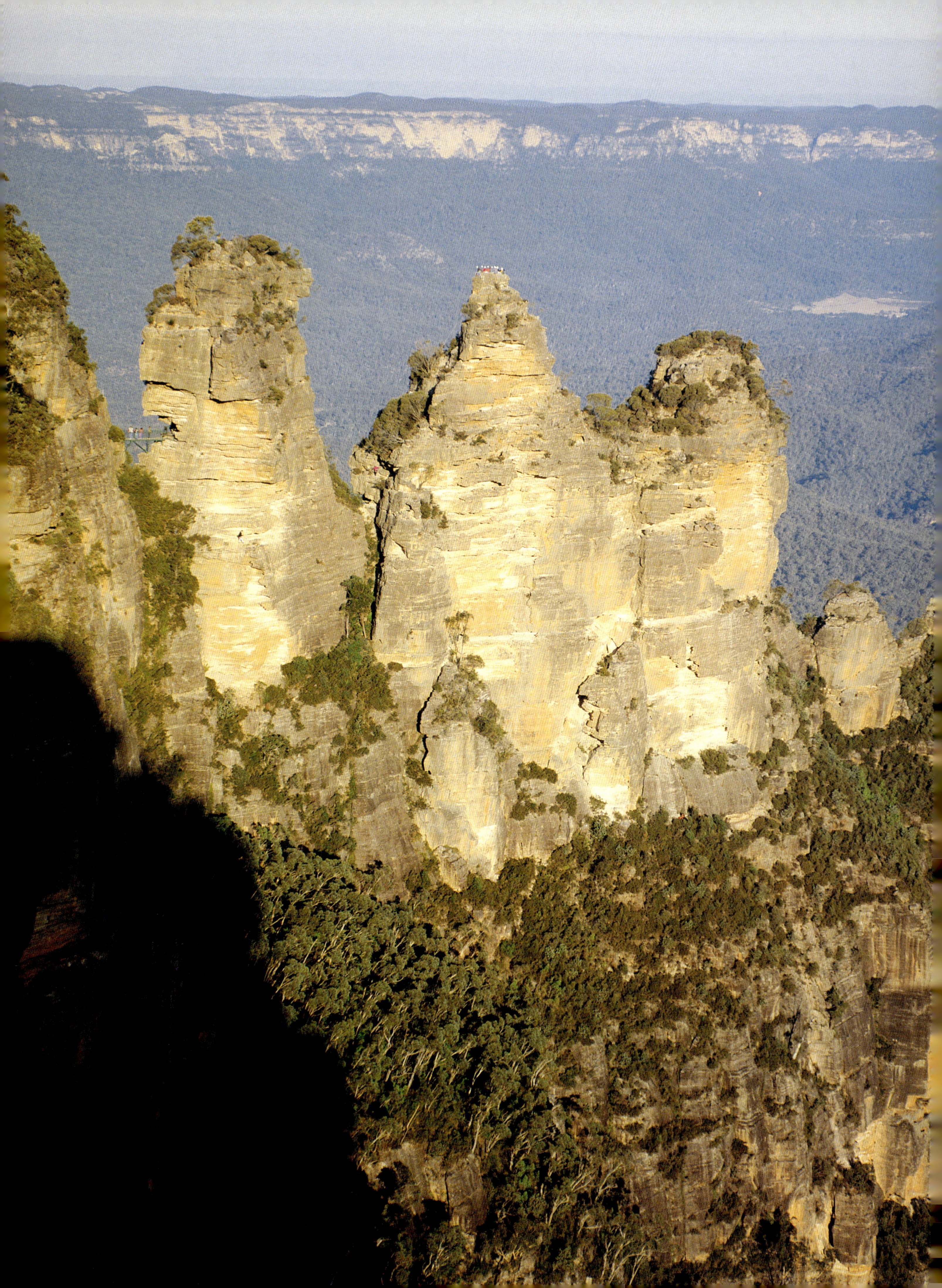

CANBERRA
AUSTRALIA'S NATIONAL CAPITAL

After Federation in 1901, the governments of the States of Australia spent nine years debating the location of a national capital before they finally agreed on a site by the Molonglo River, in southern New South Wales. American Walter Burley Griffin designed the new city of Canberra.

The eventual implementation of Burley Griffin's plan, which was finally completed with the creation of Lake Burley Griffin in the 1960s, has resulted in an open, spacious city.

In the eighty years since Canberra's foundation, a proud city of nearly 300,000 people has spread across the "limestone plains" first seen by Europeans in 1820. Where there were sheep stations, there are now elegant public buildings, broad boulevards, three city centres, three universities, colleges and institutes, memorials, research centres, museums and fine gardens. Parklands planted with native and exotic species guarantee splendid autumn colours as deciduous trees prepare to drop their leaves, then, after winter's quiet greys and greens, a brilliant burst of spring blossom.

Here, all roads lead to Capital Hill, crowned by the superb new Parliament House which was opened in 1988. The embassies of many lands contribute their own distinctive national building styles. And everywhere there is space - space to work, to play, to relax and to savour the atmosphere of this planned and gracious city.

Superb Fairy-Wren on Royal Bluebell, floral emblem of the ACT.

RIGHT, TOP TO BOTTOM: COCKINGTON GREEN IS A MASTERPIECE OF MINIATURISATION; THE CANBERRA TIMES FOUNTAIN IN THE CANBERRA CENTRE; THE TELECOM TOWER ON BLACK MOUNTAIN; BLUNDELL'S COTTAGE, BUILT IN 1858 BY ROBERT CAMPBELL OF "DUNTROON"; THE CAPTAIN COOK MEMORIAL FOUNTAIN JETS PROUDLY FROM LAKE BURLEY GRIFFIN.
OPPOSITE: A VIEW OF CANBERRA FROM MOUNT AINSLIE.

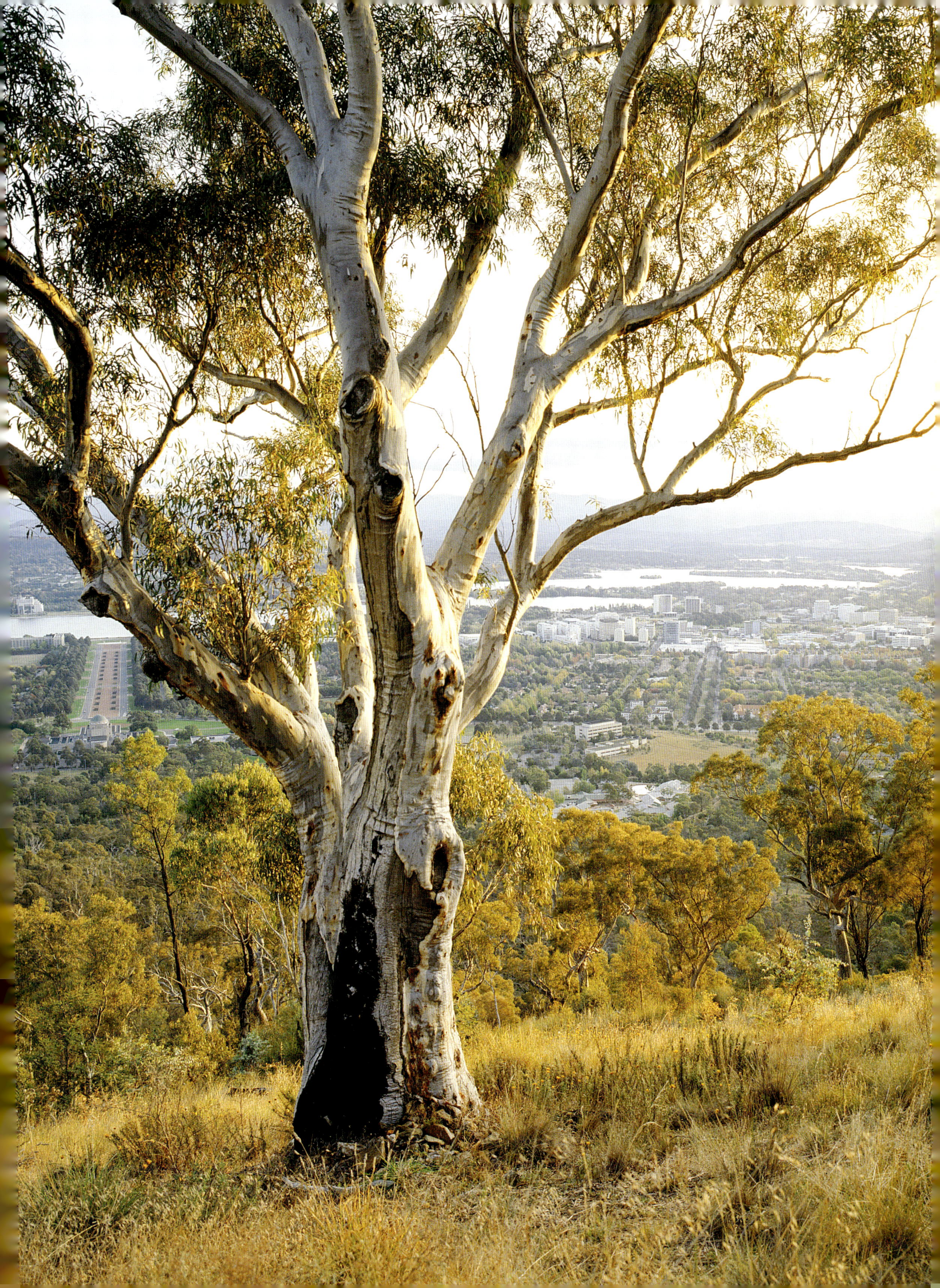

CANBERRA'S PLACES AND PEOPLE

Each of the splendid buildings pictured here has great national significance. It is also a place where many local people work. Many more people, from Australia and overseas, visit these places, to admire, to be educated and sometimes to take part in Australia's democratic processes.

TOP LEFT: THE HIGH COURT OF AUSTRALIA WAS OPENED BY QUEEN ELIZABETH II IN 1980.
CENTRE LEFT: THE NATIONAL GALLERY OF AUSTRALIA HOUSES AN EXTENSIVE COLLECTION OF ARTWORKS.
TOP RIGHT: THE NATIONAL SCIENCE AND TECHNOLOGY CENTRE HAS SIX EXHIBITION AREAS.
CENTRE RIGHT: THE AUSTRALIAN WAR MEMORIAL, OPENED IN 1941.
ABOVE: NEW PARLIAMENT HOUSE WAS OPENED IN 1988.

COLOURFUL CANBERRA

As the seasons change, the Canberra landscape undergoes transformations from the brilliant flowers of spring through the lovely colours of summer's blooms. Autumn bronzes deciduous leaves, then, in winter, native trees and evergreens dominate parks and gardens.

TOP LEFT: CANBERRA'S TREES COME FROM ALL PARTS OF THE WORLD.
CENTRE LEFT: CONIFERS BESIDE LAKE BURLEY GRIFFIN AT SUNSET.
TOP RIGHT: THE SUN SETS OVER A WINTERY LAKE BURLEY GRIFFIN.
CENTRE RIGHT: EVERLASTINGS IN THE AUSTRALIAN NATIONAL BOTANIC GARDENS.
ABOVE: CANBERRA'S COMMONWEALTH PARK DURING FLORIADE.

AUSTRALIAN WILDLIFE SYMBOLS

Kangaroo and Koala are the best-known of Australia's many fascinating native animals. Both are survivors of a time long ago, when Australia was much wetter than it is today. The climate became drier and eucalypts took the place of much of the rainforest. Kangaroos, which had been browsers eating leaves and herbs, adapted to eating grass. The Koala became a specialist in eating eucalyptus leaves.

Kangaroos and wallabies are macropods, which have strong hind legs and long feet. When moving slowly they use all four legs and their long tails as well. When moving at speed, they rise on their hindlegs and hop.

The Koala, like the kangaroos, is a marsupial, whose single young one is born tiny, naked and blind. It climbs into its mother's pouch and completes its development there. Koalas have short bodies and long arms and legs. They move slowly but surely about trees, sleep up to 19 hours of each 24 and spend most of the rest of their time eating carefully-selected eucalyptus leaves.

ABOVE: FEMALE GREY KANGAROO WITH YOUNG IN POUCH.
RIGHT: FEMALE KOALA WITH YOUNG ONE OUT OF THE POUCH BUT NOT YET INDEPENDENT.

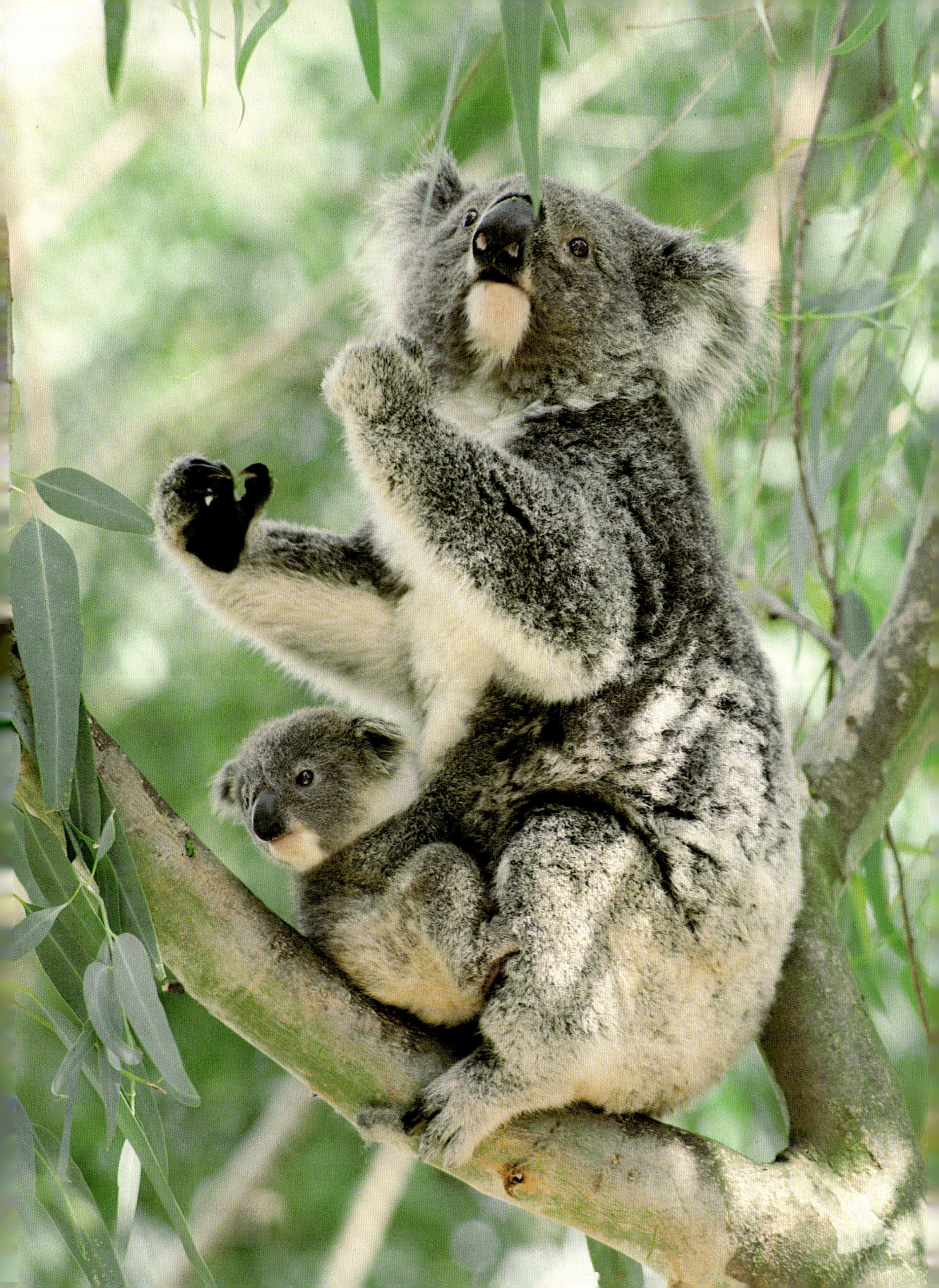

THE MURRAY
AUSTRALIA'S GREATEST RIVER

The headwaters of the Murray River rise in the High Country of Australia's Alps. This is Man From Snowy River and Kosciusko National Park country and here the Indi, the Omeo and the Geehi fuse to become the mighty Murray River, which forms the border between New South Wales and Victoria as it flows 2530 kilometres to join the Southern Ocean at Encounter Bay.

The Murray and its tributaries drain more than one million square kilometres of Australia to the west of the Great Dividing Range. On its long odyssey, the Murray passes from the high Alps, with their winter snows and summer wildflowers, through forested ranges, fertile farmlands, orchards, green pastures and drier regions, where its waters are essential to support human activity. Many hectares of land are irrigated by the Murray. It directly affects the lives of around 250,000 of Australia's people and influences many more indirectly.

ABOVE: THE MIGHTY MURRAY INVADES ITS FLOODPLAIN.
BELOW: SUNRISE ON THE MURRAY FLATS.
OPPOSITE: A PADDLEWHEELER MOORED AT ECHUCA, ON THE MURRAY RIVER.

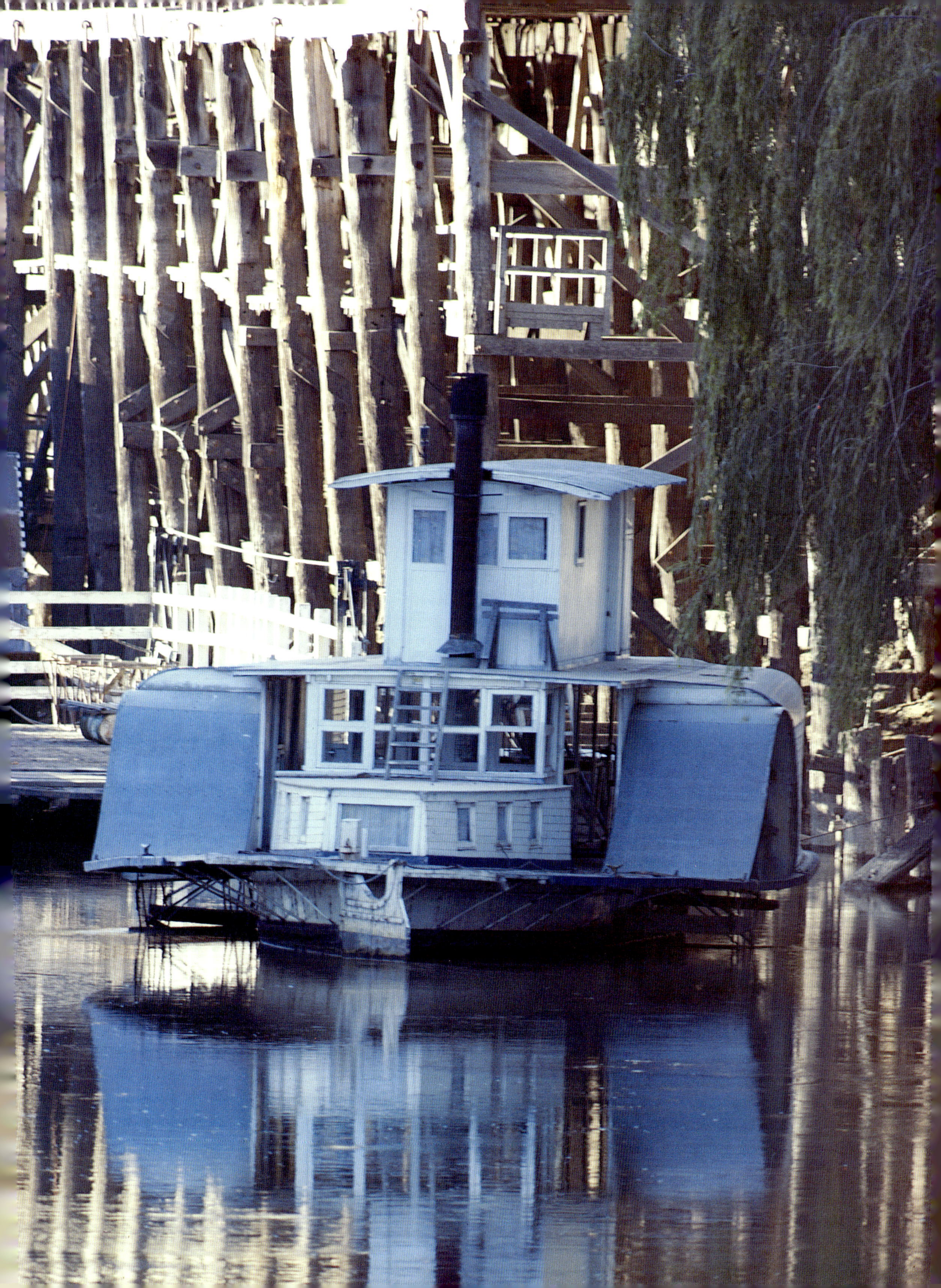

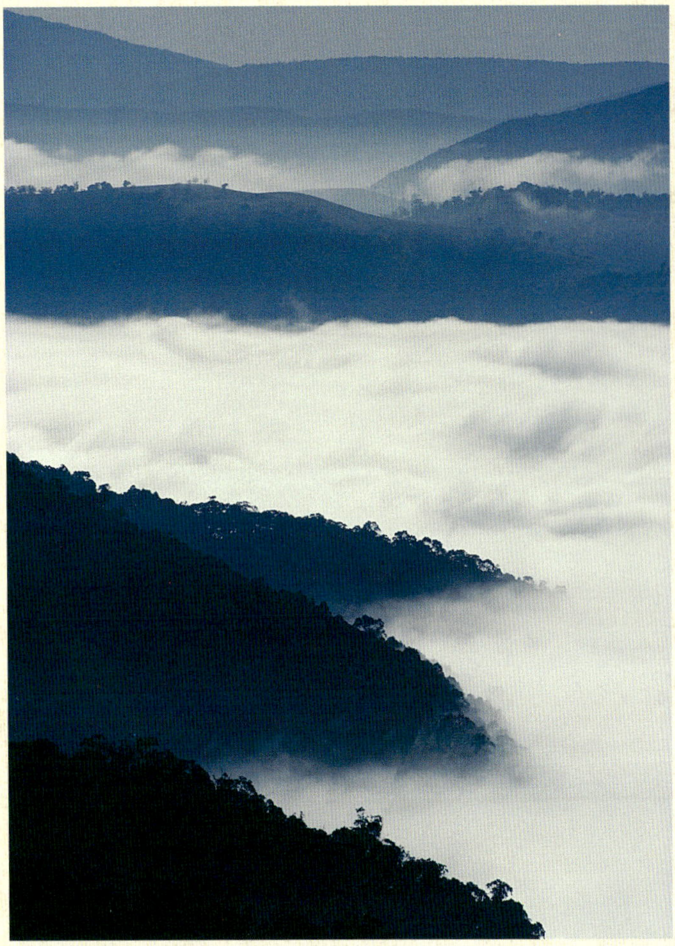
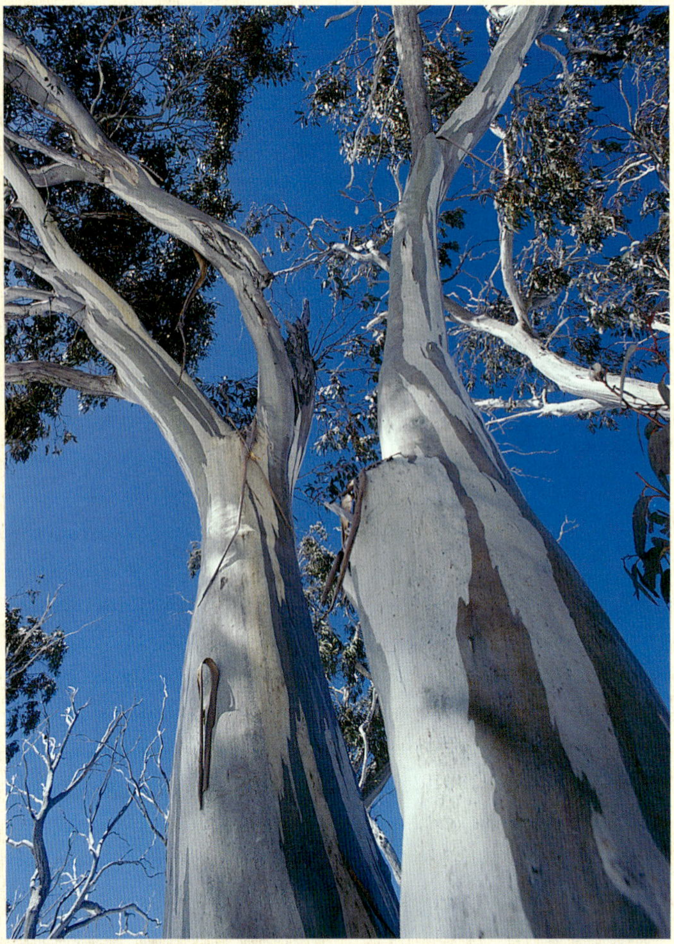
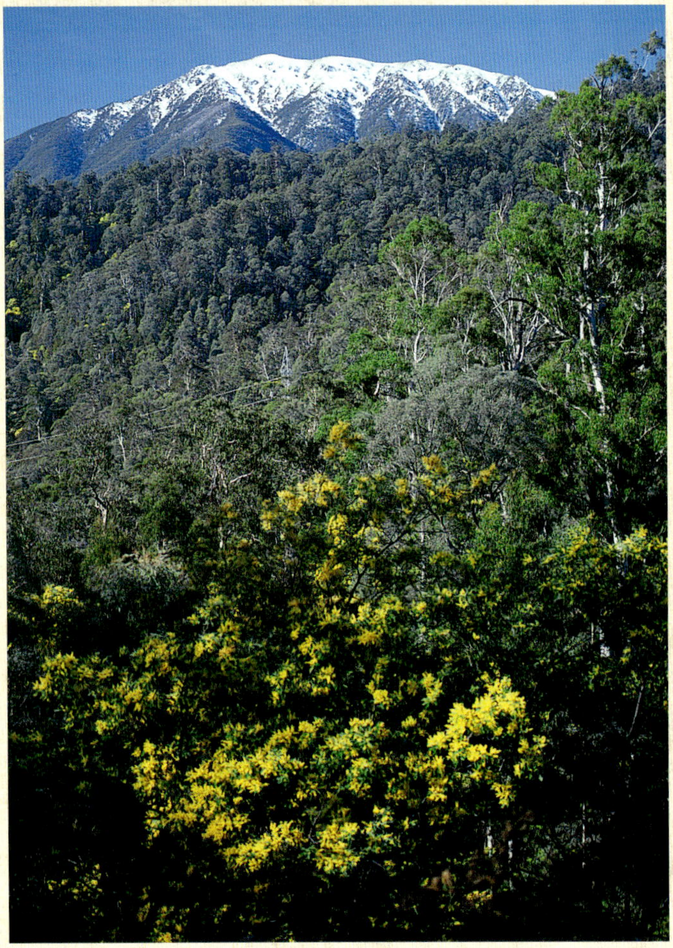
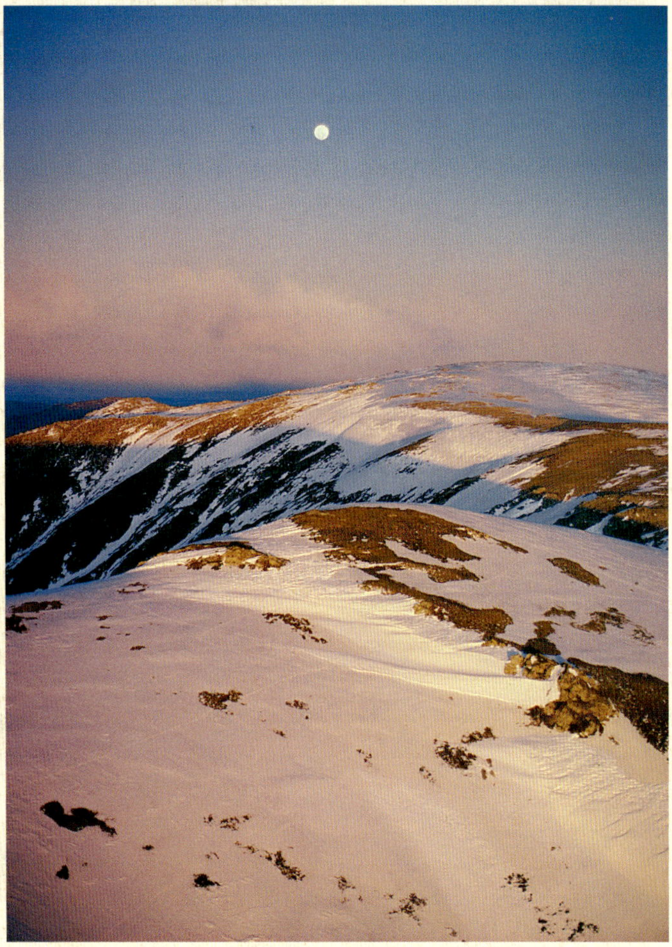

THE AUSTRALIAN ALPS
A YEAR-ROUND PLAYGROUND

The Australian Alps were formed beneath an ancient sea, laid down as sediments of volcanic ash, lava and sand, which movements of the earth's crust eventually thrust above the ocean. The range was eroded, then was submerged again and for another 100 million years was covered with new sediment. Some 350 million years ago, the mountains were pushed above the sea's surface once more. Sixty million years ago, another convulsion elevated the peaks up to 4000 metres above sea level. Since then, the forces of erosion have steadily worn away the rock and created plateaus, gorges and cliffs.

In winter, the Australian Alps contain more skiable snow than Switzerland. Though the skiing season officially opens in June and closes in October, the mountains attract walkers, climbers and holiday-makers all year round. Summer, which sees the heathlands of the High Country colourful with wildflowers, is particularly lovely in the Alps.

OPPOSITE: SCENES FROM THE AUSTRALIAN ALPS.
CLOCKWISE FROM TOP LEFT: MIST-FILLED VALLEYS; SNOW GUMS; MOONLIT SNOWY PEAKS; SPRINGTIME BLOOMS.
RIGHT ABOVE AND BELOW: THE AUSTRALIAN ALPS, A WINTER WONDERLAND.

MELBOURNE
AND THE GARDEN STATE OF VICTORIA

On 8 June 1835, Tasmania's John Batman "purchased" the site of Melbourne from a group of Aborigines. The "treaty" was later declared invalid, but settlement went ahead anyway. In the 1850s, riches from gold financed the construction of many distinguished buildings. Gold also provided the means whereby Surveyor Robert Hoddle's plan for the city was realised. Today Melbourne is called "the Garden City" with good reason, its character set by its gardens, its wide boulevards shaded by beautiful trees and its winding Yarra River, flowing between green banks and under many bridges.

Melbourne is a multi-faced metropolis. It is a dedicated centre of the arts, which has raised the code of Australian Rules football to cult status. It contains large ethnic communities, whose children grow up with the best of many inheritances. It is a city which has turned outdoor living into a fine art. Walk across Princes Bridge to Southgate, with its marvellous restaurants, or take a few steps further to the Victorian Arts Centre and National Gallery of Victoria, or cross St Kilda Road to Queen Victoria Gardens ... or just take a tram ride and savour the unique atmosphere of this queen of Australian cities.

ABOVE: MELBOURNE VIEWED FROM ST KILDA PIER.
BELOW LEFT: THE STATELY SAINT MICHAEL'S CHURCH AND THE MODERN HYATT HOTEL.
BELOW RIGHT: MELBOURNE CENTRAL COMPLEX SHELTERS AN HISTORIC SHOT TOWER.
OPPOSITE: FLINDERS STREET STATION, CENTRE OF A NOTABLE TRANSPORT SYSTEM.

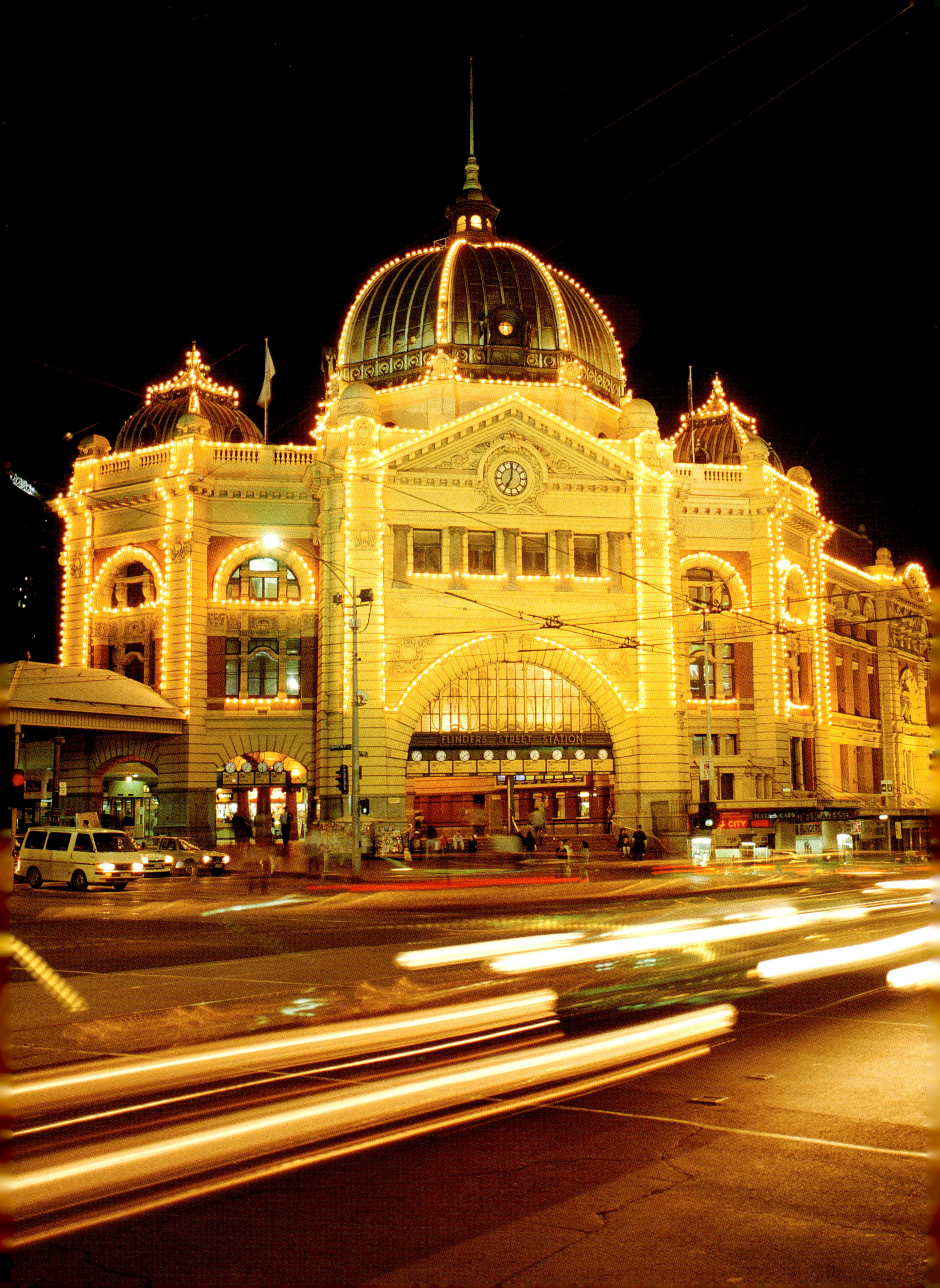
FLINDERS STREET STATION

TOP LEFT AND CLOCKWISE: GROUNDS AND SPIRE OF THE VICTORIAN ARTS CENTRE; SATURDAY AFTERNOON IN THE MELBOURNE SUBURBS; ONE OF MELBOURNE'S FAMOUS TRAMS; BATHING BOXES AT BRIGHTON BEACH; FERRY ON THE YARRA RIVER; THE SHRINE OF REMEMBRANCE.

OPPOSITE: A FOOTBRIDGE LEADS ACROSS THE YARRA AT SOUTHGATE
INSET LEFT TO RIGHT: THE YARRA FLOWS PLACIDLY UNDER PRINCES BRIDGE; SPRINGTIME DISPLAY IN THE CONSERVATORY, FITZROY GARDENS; CAPTAIN COOK'S COTTAGE IN FITZROY GARDENS.

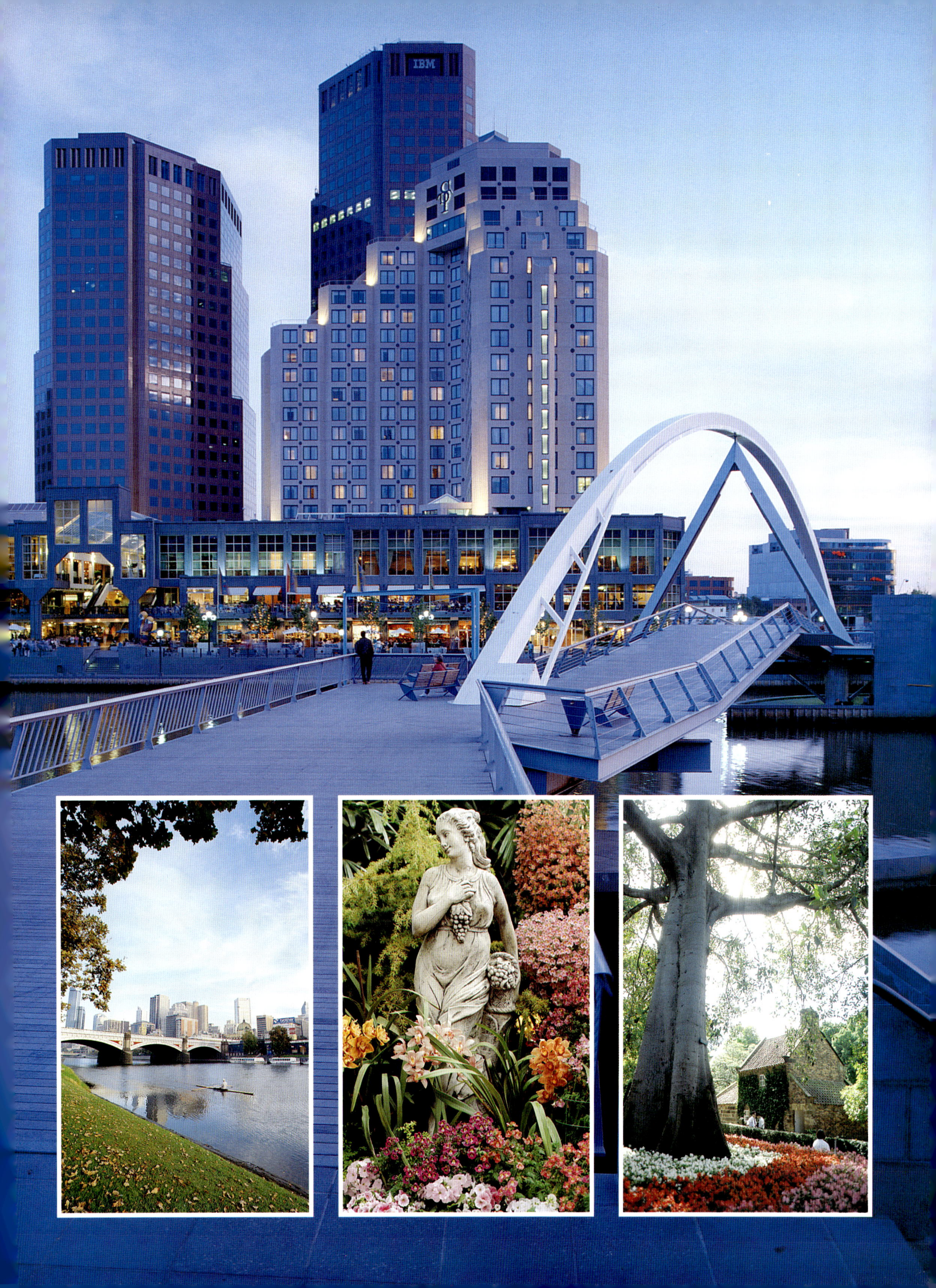
IBM

ABOVE: THE TWELVE APOSTLES ARE AMONGST MANY SCENIC ATTRACTIONS ACCESSED BY THE GREAT OCEAN ROAD.
BELOW: HOPETOUN FALLS, ONE OF THE MAGICAL WATERFALLS FOUND IN THE OTWAY RANGES.

ABOVE: VICTORIAN KOALAS ARE LARGER AND HAVE THICKER FUR THAN NORTHERN MEMBERS OF THE SPECIES.
BELOW: THE NIGHTLY "PARADE" OF THE LITTLE PENGUINS IS SEEN AT PHILLIP ISLAND AND OTHER BEACHES.

HOBART

AND THE ISLAND STATE OF TASMANIA

Standing on top of Mount Wellington, the viewer is 1,270 metres above the Derwent River and the city of Hobart, capital of Tasmania. To the east is Sullivans Cove, where, in 1804, Governor David Collins, with 358 men, 39 women and 36 children established a settlement. Hobart's waterfront knew wild days in the early nineteenth century, when whalers and sealers docked there. The island is proud of its history and reminders of the convict days still exist in the ruins of Port Arthur penal settlement on the Tasman Peninsula and in roads, bridges and public buildings in towns such as Richmond.

Tasmania contains many wilderness areas, ranging from stark and rugged mountain peaks to unspoiled coast, from verdant rainforest to the glory of wild rivers. The cool, pleasant climate and the warm hospitality of the Tasmanians combine to make this southern State a true "holiday island".

ABOVE LEFT TO RIGHT: HOBART IS A MARITIME CITY; THE RUINS OF PORT ARTHUR PENAL SETTLEMENT; CONVICT-BUILT BRIDGE AT RICHMOND.
BELOW LEFT TO RIGHT: CRADLE MOUNTAIN-LAKE ST CLAIR NATIONAL PARK; TASMANIAN DEVIL; SOUTHWEST CAPE.
OPPOSITE TOP LEFT AND CLOCKWISE: HOBART, CAPITAL OF TASMANIA; BATHURST HARBOUR, SOUTHWEST NATIONAL PARK; WREST POINT CASINO IN HOBART; THE MAGNIFICENT ARTHUR RANGES.
FOLLOWING PAGES: RUSSELL FALLS, IN MOUNT FIELD NATIONAL PARK, WHICH IS ONLY 80 KILOMETRES FROM HOBART.

25

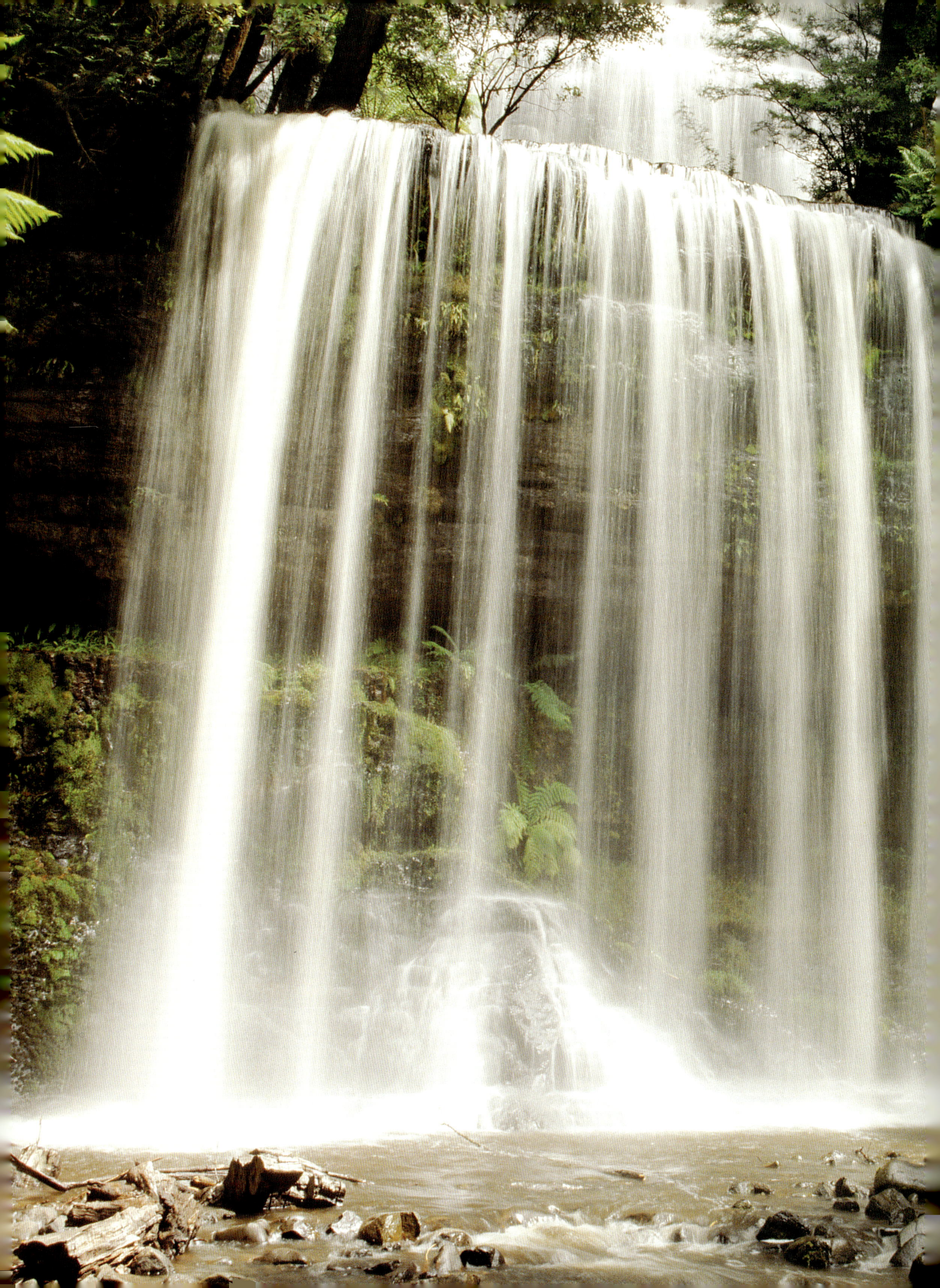

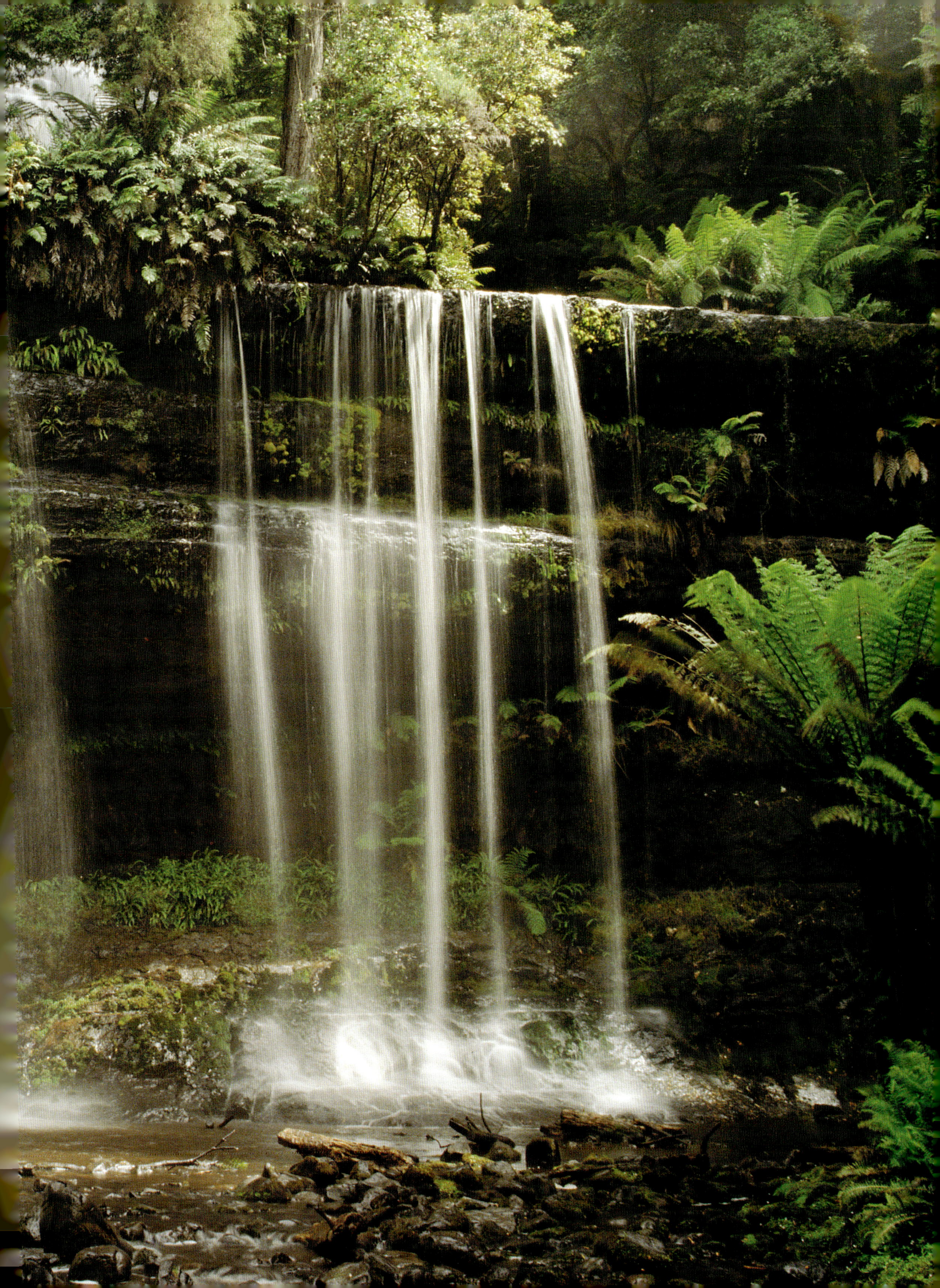

ADELAIDE

AND THE FESTIVAL STATE OF SOUTH AUSTRALIA

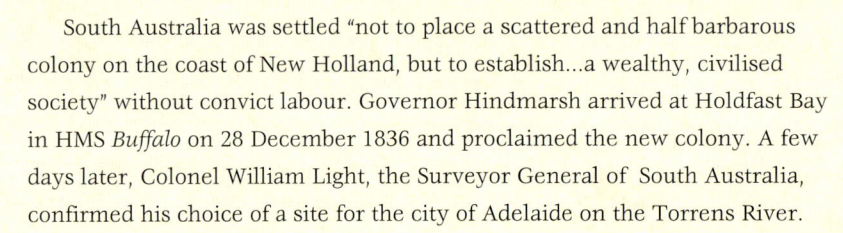

South Australia was settled "not to place a scattered and half barbarous colony on the coast of New Holland, but to establish...a wealthy, civilised society" without convict labour. Governor Hindmarsh arrived at Holdfast Bay in HMS *Buffalo* on 28 December 1836 and proclaimed the new colony. A few days later, Colonel William Light, the Surveyor General of South Australia, confirmed his choice of a site for the city of Adelaide on the Torrens River.

Today, the lovely city of Adelaide is set in parklands planned by Colonel Light. It has wide tree-lined streets, many stately public buildings and enjoys a magnificent Mediterranean climate. The Festival Centre complex on the south bank of Torrens Lake showcases the arts at Adelaide's famous biennial Festival.

An influx of German migrants to the State in the nineteenth century led to the pre-eminence of South Australia in vine cultivation and wine production. The southern seas are rich, the southeast of the State is wondrously fertile, the scenery of the Flinders Ranges and southern coasts is magnificent. The State of South Australia provides a fine setting for its beautiful capital city.

Crimson Chat on Sturt's Desert Pea, floral emblem of South Australia.

ABOVE: SYMPHONY IN ELDER PARK AT THE ADELAIDE FESTIVAL OF ARTS.
BELOW LEFT AND RIGHT: THE HOUSES OF PARLIAMENT; ADELAIDE'S RAILWAY STATION AND CASINO.
OPPOSITE: ADELAIDE FROM THE AIR.

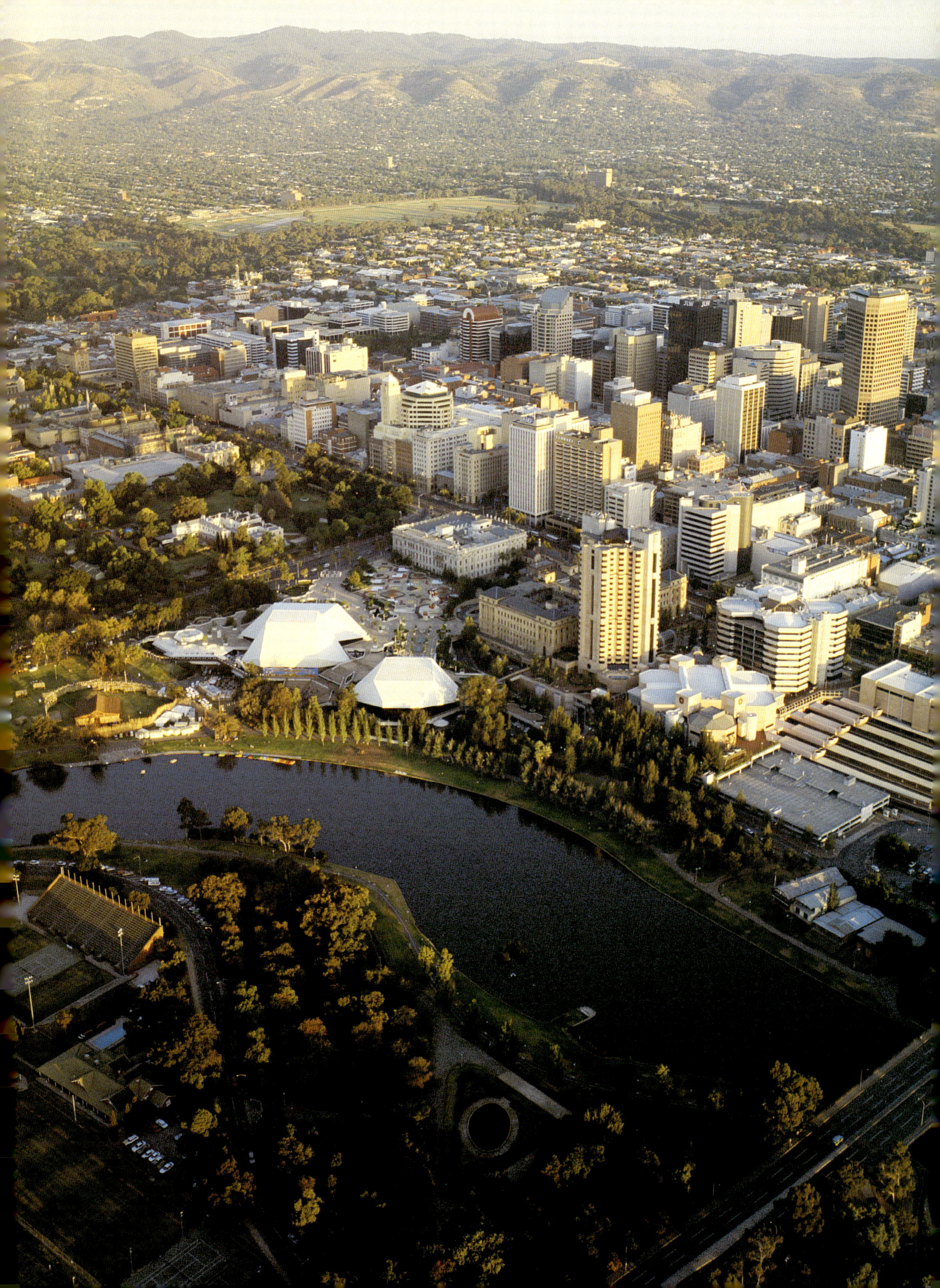

ABOVE LEFT AND RIGHT: THE VICTORIA SQUARE FOUNTAIN IS THE WORK OF JOHN S. DOWIE; ADELAIDE VIEWED ACROSS TORRENS LAKE.
BELOW: SCULPTURES IN THE SPACIOUS PLAZA OF THE ADELAIDE FESTIVAL CENTRE.

TOP LEFT AND RIGHT: THE NORTHEASTERN DESERT AFTER RAIN; REMARKABLE ROCKS ON KANGAROO ISLAND.
CENTRE LEFT AND RIGHT: STURT'S DESERT PEA, FLORAL EMBLEM OF SOUTH AUSTRALIA; AUSTRALIAN PELICANS ON THE COORONG.
ABOVE LEFT AND RIGHT: MURRAY RIVER CLIFFS NEAR WALKER FLAT; LANDSCAPE IN THE FLINDERS RANGES, NORTH OF ADELAIDE.

32

THE RED CENTRE

From the top of a tumble of granite tors overlooking Alice Springs, the viewer can see the beautifully-restored telegraph repeater station, built in 1871 near the Alice Spring on the Todd River. Downstream, the Todd winds through the bustling town, which is accessible by road, air and by the ever-popular Ghan Railway. On rare occasions, the Todd becomes a deep, raging torrent, powerful enough to have cut the incredible Heavitree Gap through the rugged quartzites of the MacDonnell Ranges, which run for some 400 kilometres across central Australia. Numerous rivers and creeks have made great gashes through their ancient rocks. Once seen, these gorges are never forgotten: Simpsons Gap with its colony of rock wallabies; Serpentine Gorge, with its deep, cold water; Standley Chasm, where the midday sun colours the rock to the hue of molten lava; the grandeur of Ormiston Gorge; the deep reds and purples of Redbank and Trephina Gorges - all are scenic wonders.

Approximately 440 kilometres southwest of Alice Springs is Uluru National Park, which encloses the massive monolith of Uluru and the wonderful domes of Kata Tjuta. The remarkable rocks known as the Devils Marbles are about 400 kilometres north of "the Alice", near the Stuart Highway.

OPPOSITE: **LEFT AND CLOCKWISE:** THE COLOURS OF AUSTRALIA'S RED CENTRE; THIS TELEGRAPH STATION WAS BUILT IN 1871; THE WEDGE-TAILED EAGLE FLIES HIGH OVER THE RED CENTRE; ALICE SPRINGS, A HUMAN FOCUS IN THE RED CENTRE.
ABOVE: THE GIGANTIC BULK OF KATA TJUTA CAN BE GAUGED BY THE SIZE OF ITS ADMIRERS.
BELOW LEFT TO RIGHT: LEARNING ABOUT ULURU; CLIMBING ULURU; EXPLORING THE RIM OF KINGS CANYON.

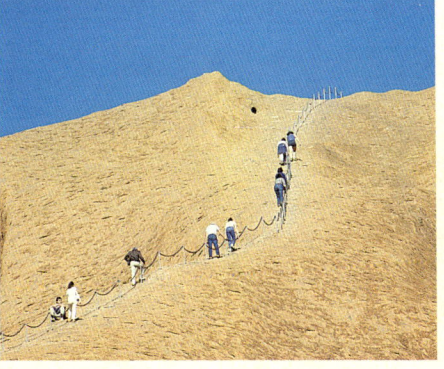

TOP LEFT AND CLOCKWISE: ORMISTON GORGE AND POUND NATIONAL PARK, IN THE WEST MACDONNELL RANGES; CHAMBERS PILLAR; KINGS CANYON; FINKE GORGE HAS MANY SPECTACULAR CLIFFS.

ABOVE: THE DOMES OF KATA TJUTA RISE 32 KILOMETRES WEST OF ULURU.
BELOW: THE DEVILS MARBLES ARE HUGE ROUNDED BOULDERS STANDING BESIDE THE STUART HIGHWAY.

ULURU, SYMBOL OF AUSTRALIA

Six hundred million years ago, there was a mighty mountain range in what is now central Australia. Today, its eroded remnants form Uluru and Kata Tjuta. Aboriginal stories tell that the Rock was once a giant sandhill about which moved ancestors. Today, the spirits of these ancestors still reside there.

If you visit Uluru, you will be infinitely richer in experience if you can tune your eyes and ears to the remarkable stories existing all about you. Most rewarding is to visit the Rock between autumn and late spring and to walk the ten kilometres around its base, preferably with a knowledgeable guide. See the changes of colour and feel the coolness at Kantju Gorge and Mutitjulu waterholes. Imagine ceremonies by firelight at the foot of Uluru. Listen to birdsong and watch the play of kestrels sweeping on slender curved wings across the stone faces. This is a place of power. Then visit Kata Tjuta and walk into awe-inspiring Olga Gorge and experience the serenity of the Valley of the Winds.

ABOVE: ULURU IS THE EXPOSED PORTION OF A MASSIVE ROCK.
OPPOSITE: THE EVER-CHANGING ASPECTS OF ULURU.
FOLLOWING PAGES: ULURU, A MONOLITH WHICH MEANS MANY THINGS TO MANY PEOPLE.

37

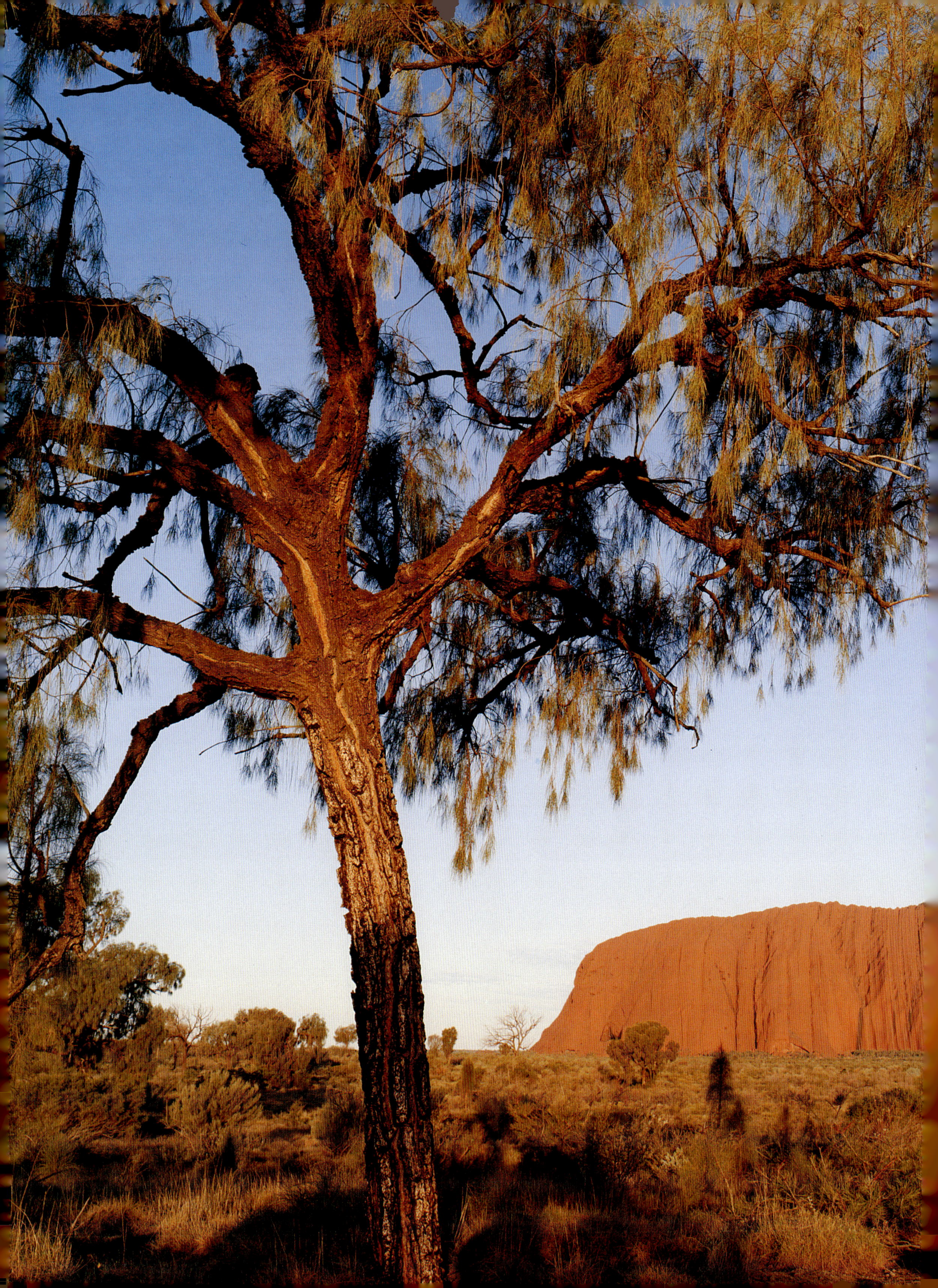

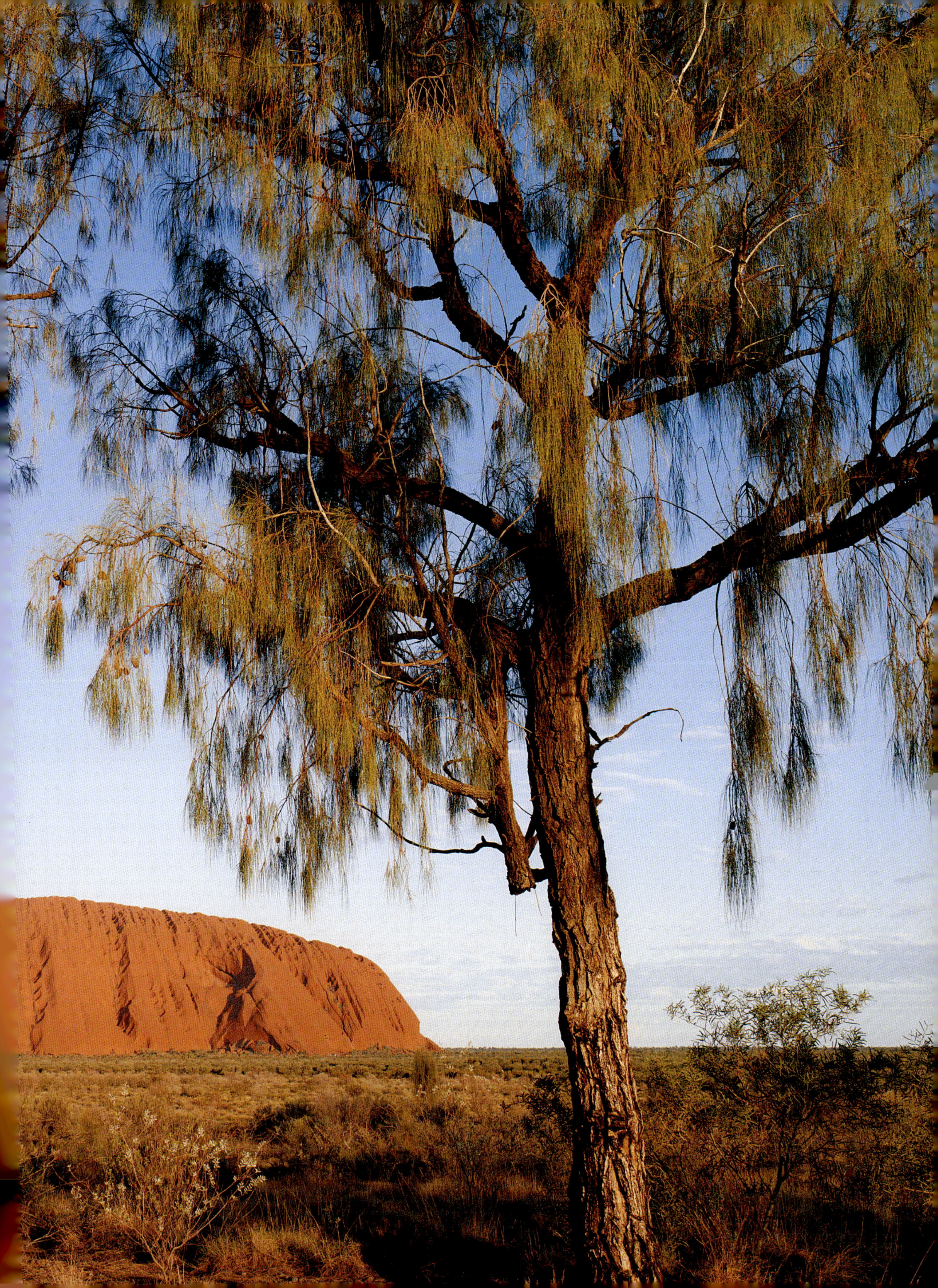

OUTBACK AUSTRALIA
AND THE STOCKMAN'S HALL OF FAME

The country around Longreach in central Queensland is typical in many ways of Australia's Outback. This, like so many places across the continent, is an area of wide open spaces, subject to periodic droughts, sometimes followed by flooding rains.

On these plains, for months on end, cattle can be seen belly-deep in an endless sea of Mitchell and Flinders grasses. As the pasture is cropped down a trifle, tens of thousands of sheep come to view. Life goes on - mustering, branding, shearing, sending stock to market. Then, with the early summer storms, comes the lightning. Fires roar across the plains, consuming grass, animals and sometimes homesteads. When it is all over, black-faced, red-eyed fire-fighters gulp down pannikins of strong tea before counting the cost. All will pray for a good wet season, but all too often the rains will be late or scanty. Dust hazes will follow stock straggling to and from water and searching for feed. Winton, Longreach, Barcaldine and Blackall will see fewer and fewer graziers in town spending their reserves. But everyone hangs on, looking forward to the good times, when the rains come again and wool prices go through the shearing shed roof and new beef markets open up.

This is a scenario repeated all over Australia's outback. It's a tough land, but loved by those who live in its vastness.

ABOVE: THE BIRDSVILLE HOTEL, ONE OF AUSTRALIA'S LONELIEST PUBS.
BELOW: COMING INTO THE STRAIGHT AT AN OUTBACK RACE MEETING.
OPPOSITE: THE STOCKMAN'S HALL OF FAME AND OUTBACK HERITAGE CENTRE, LONGREACH.
INSET: STOCKMEN RIDE INTO THE DAWN TO MUSTER CATTLE.

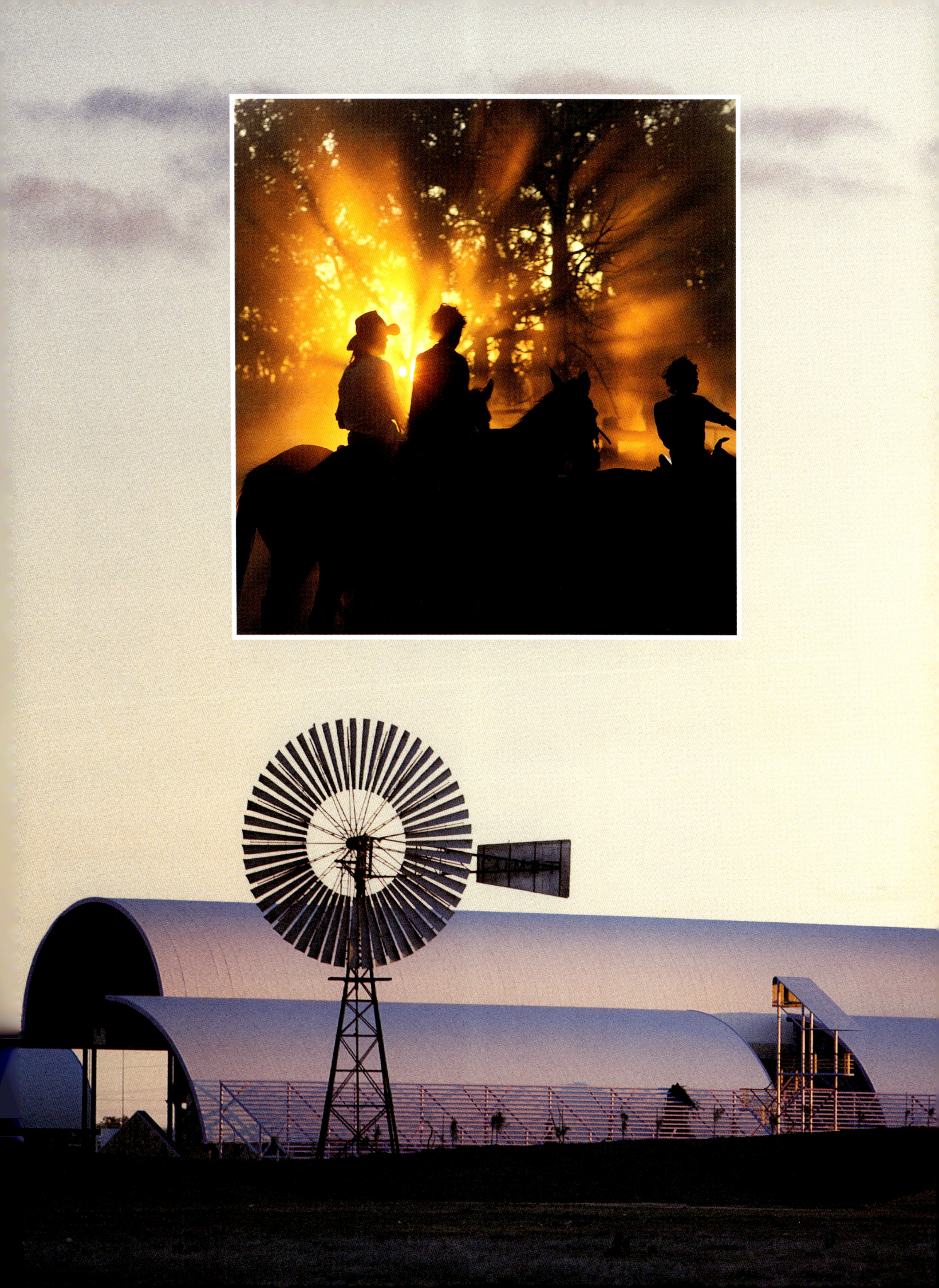

SHEEP HAVE BEEN THE FOUNDATION OF MUCH OF AUSTRALIA'S RURAL PROSPERITY.

ALL HANDS ARE NEEDED TO MUSTER THE BEASTS IN AUSTRALIA'S CATTLE COUNTRY.

44

PERTH

AND THE WILDFLOWER STATE OF WESTERN AUSTRALIA

On Christmas Day, 1826, in order to forestall action by France, England's Major Lockyer and forty soldiers and convicts from the brig *Amity* established the town of Albany on Princess Royal Harbour, King George Sound, on the south coast of Western Australia. Perth, the capital of the State, was founded in 1829 further north, on the Swan River. The settlement was not immediately prosperous and in 1850 the British Government sent in a convict labour force which constructed many public amenities before transportation was abolished. The gold rushes of the 1890s made Perth and Fremantle into cities of note. For the past hundred years, gold, iron ore, nickel, bauxite, petroleum and diamonds have outstripped rural industries in maintaining prosperity in Western Australia.

Leisure time is never difficult to fill in this huge State, with its many climates and scenic attractions. Springtime brings the magnificent wildflowers of the southwest. In summer it is time to explore the southwest and southern coast. Autumn and winter send the adventurous travellers north along excellent roads to the scenic Pilbara, the Pearl Coast and the rugged Kimberley Division.

OPPOSITE: TOP LEFT AND CLOCKWISE: BESIDE THE SWAN RIVER; THE SWAN RIVER IS PERTH'S PLAYGROUND; FREMANTLE, PORT AT THE MOUTH OF THE SWAN RIVER; KINGS PARK OVERLOOKS PERTH CITY; HAY STREET MALL WITH TOWN HALL IN THE BACKGROUND; PERTH AT NIGHT, THE NARROWS BRIDGE AND THE SWAN RIVER.

ABOVE LEFT TO RIGHT: AUSTRALIAN PELICAN; MANGLES' KANGAROO PAW IS THE STATE'S FLORAL EMBLEM; THE NUMBAT, A RARE MARSUPIAL OF THE SOUTHWEST.
BELOW: THE PINNACLES, PILLARS OF LIMESTONE IN NAMBUNG NATIONAL PARK.

WESTERN AUSTRALIA IS A FLORAL WONDERLAND.
TOP LEFT AND CLOCKWISE: FRINGED LILY; YELLOW FLAG; SCARLET BANKSIA; EVERLASTING DAISIES; MOTTLECAH.

WESTERN AUSTRALIA IS A STATE OFFERING GREAT DIVERSITY.
TOP LEFT AND CLOCKWISE: WAVE ROCK AT HYDEN; KIMBERLEY WATERFALLS; ROEBUCK BAY, BROOME;
MUSTERING IN THE KIMBERLEY; MEETING BOTTLENOSED DOLPHINS AT MONKEY MIA, SHARK BAY.

48

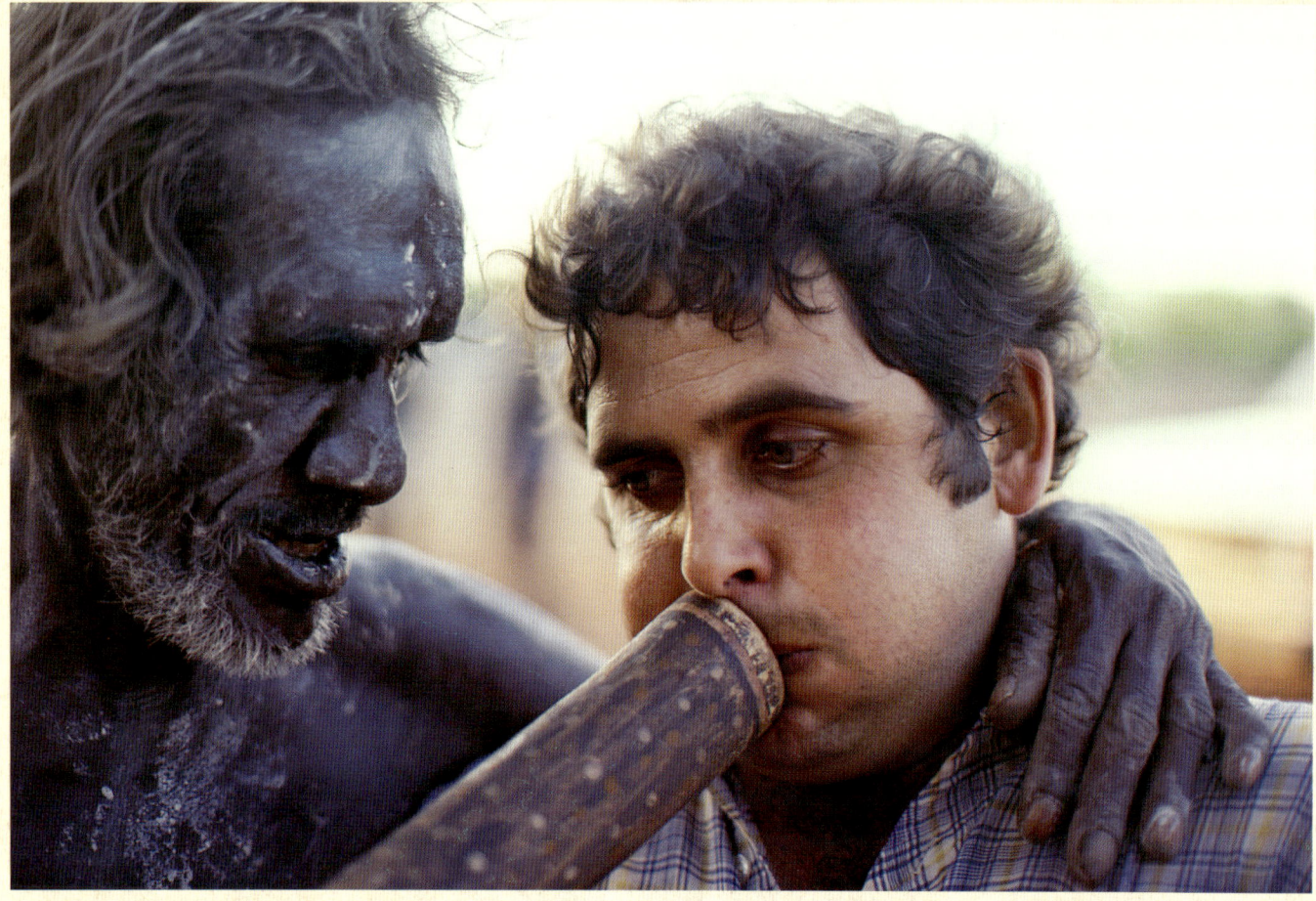

DARWIN
AND THE TROPICAL TOP END

"It is a strange fact that all who have lived there for any lengthened period, deeply regret leaving it, and have always the craving to get back again...", reflected Alfred Searcy of Darwin in 1909, after spending 14 years there as Customs Inspector. Darwin in those days was a frontier town of pearlers, buffalo hunters and crocodile shooters. Today, viewing the boutiques along Smith Street Mall, or attending a concert in the Performing Arts Centre, it is difficult to imagine those turbulent times. However, the tradition of the frontier town is preserved in historic buildings along the Esplanade and in displays at the magnificent Museum and Art Gallery on Bullocky Point.

Two hundred and fifty kilometres east of Darwin is Kakadu National Park, whose spectacular sandstone escarpment contains unique Aboriginal art galleries. Rainforests, bushland, superb wet-season waterfalls and bird-filled wetlands capture the imagination of all who visit Kakadu.

A shorter drive from Darwin, Litchfield National Park has waterfalls dropping into pools ringed by rainforest. South of Darwin, Katherine Gorge slices its way through an extension of the Arnhem Land sandstones. Here, deep, green waters reflect the sheer walls of the gorge, while on sandbanks, Freshwater Crocodiles lie sunning, or shelter in the shade of figs, paperbarks and pandanus trees.

OPPOSITE: TOP LEFT AND CLOCKWISE: JIM JIM FALLS, KAKADU NATIONAL PARK; AN AERIAL VIEW OF DARWIN; DIAMOND BEACH CASINO, DARWIN; THE ABORIGINAL PEOPLE OF THE TOP END ARE WILLING TO SHARE THEIR CULTURE; TWIN FALLS, KAKADU NATIONAL PARK; KATHERINE GORGE, NITMILUK NATIONAL PARK; FLORENCE FALLS, LITCHFIELD NATIONAL PARK;

ABOVE: KAKADU NATIONAL PARK. **LEFT TO RIGHT:** UBIRR SANDSTONE COUNTRY; ABORIGINAL ROCK ART; NOURLANGIE ROCK.
BELOW LEFT AND RIGHT: SUNSET MAGIC IN THE TOP END WETLANDS.

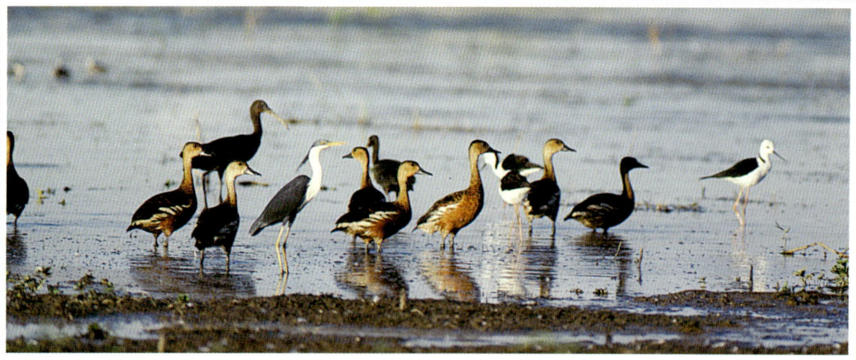

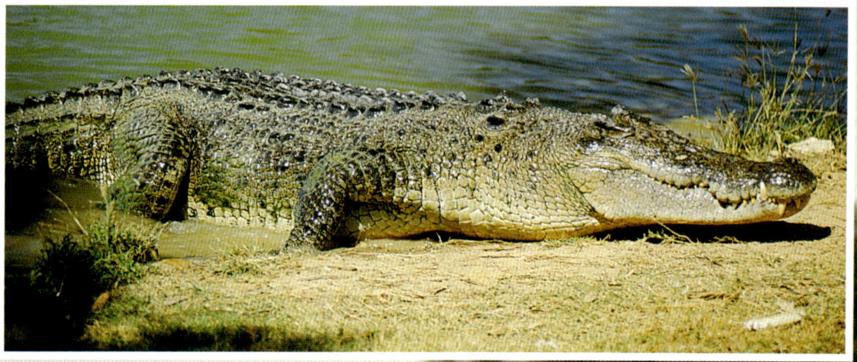

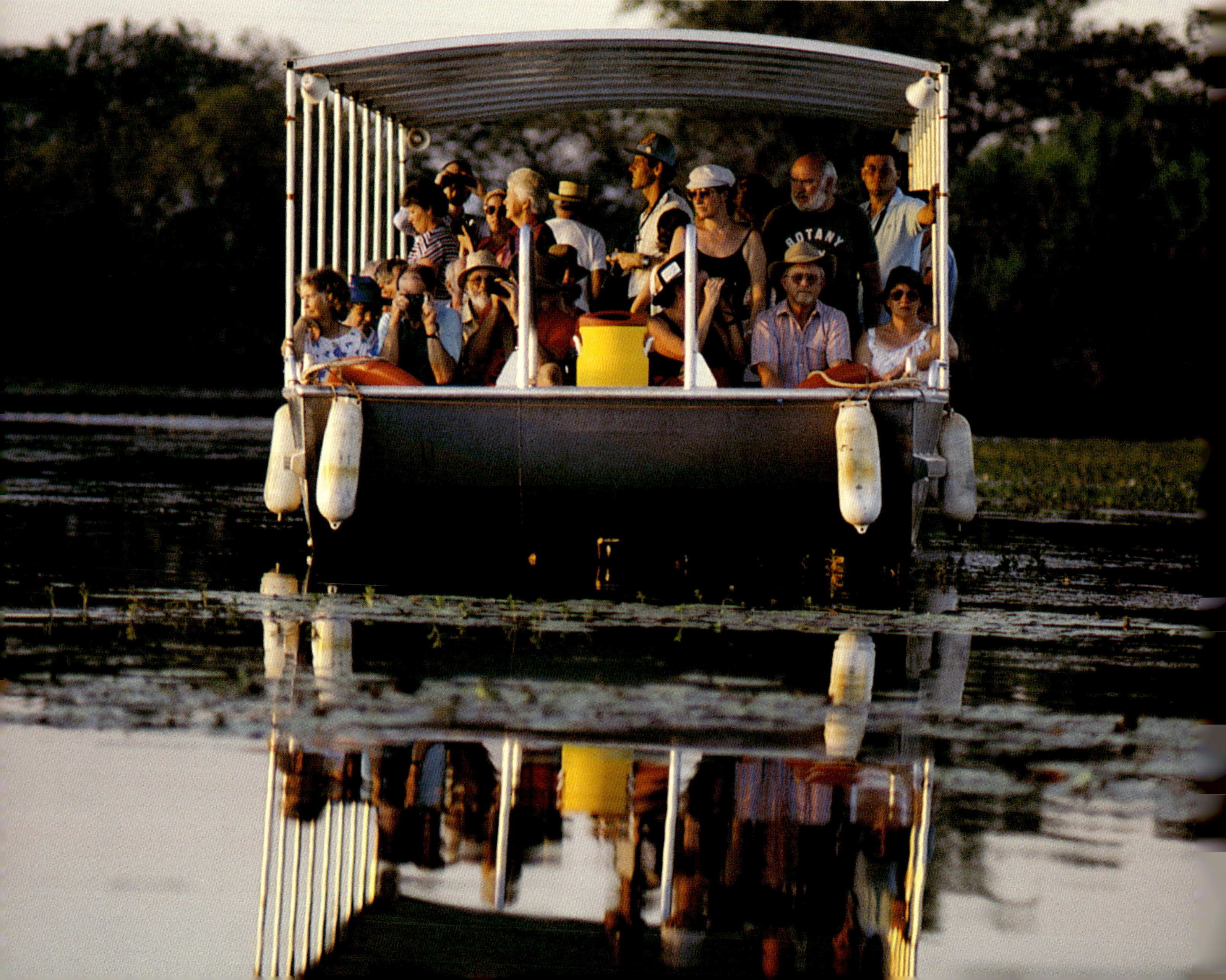
BOTANY

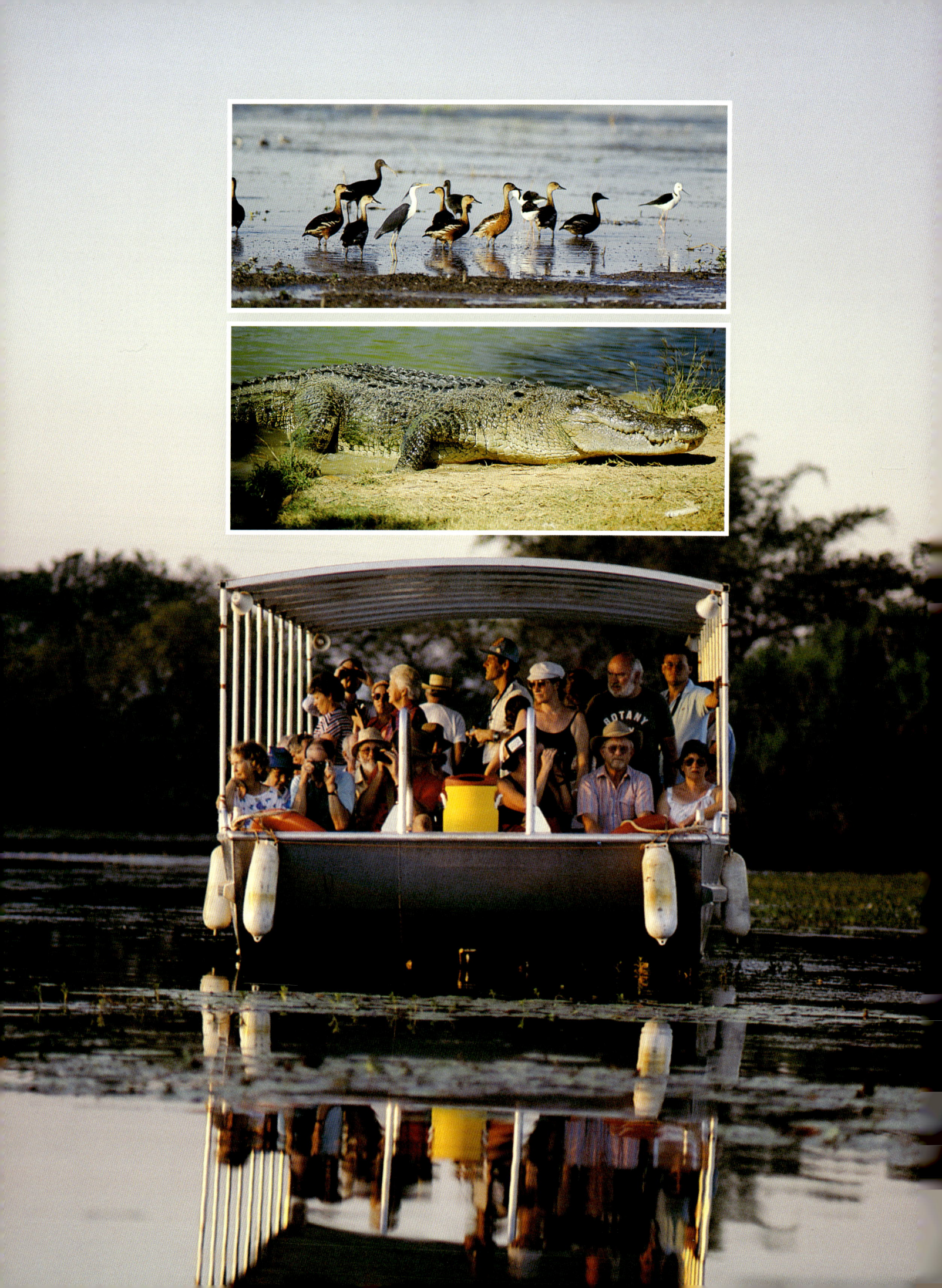

TOP END WETLANDS
HOME TO WILDLIFE

During the Dry season in the Top End, the wildlife which finds food near or in water becomes concentrated on rivers, billabongs and lagoons. Once the Wet breaks, fish, frogs and insects build up rapidly in numbers in the coastal wetlands and waterbirds spread out and breed prolifically. The country is paradise for birdwatchers, but, when studying waterbirds, it is well to remember that the Top End waterways are home to the Saltwater Crocodile, a large and efficient predator, as well as to the Freshwater Crocodile, a smaller reptile which eats mainly aquatic animals such as fish.

OPPOSITE: MAIN PICTURE: WATCHING WILDLIFE AT YELLOW WATER BILLABONG.
INSET ABOVE AND BELOW: A MIXED GROUP OF WATERBIRDS AT YELLOW WATER; SALTWATER CROCODILE.
ABOVE TOP LEFT AND CLOCKWISE: PIED HERON; NANKEEN NIGHT-HERON; MAGPIE GEESE, STRAW-NECKED IBIS; BURDEKIN DUCKS; AUSTRALIAN PELICAN; COMB-CRESTED JACANA; AUSTRALIAN DARTER; JABIRU.

THE GREAT BARRIER REEF
A MARINE WONDERLAND

The Great Barrier Reef is really a series of reefs stretching for nearly 2,000 kilometres along the edge of Queensland's continental shelf.

Around 400 different kinds of soft and hard corals form the building blocks of the Reef. Some of these corals thrive on the turbulent line where the continental shelf plunges into the deep, some like calmer waters, some favour shallows with bright light, some prefer warmer water, and others flourish in cooler conditions. Corals grow best in warm, well-lit, clean, ever-circulating seawater, which brings them oxygen, nutrients and the calcium from which the coral animals or polyps build their homes.

These tiny coral polyps exist in uncountable numbers and in many shapes and colours. They form partnerships with algae, which are able to use sunlight to make energy. The limestone homes of colonies of polyps form an incredibly complex reef, which houses a great variety of other marine animals.

So the reef is formed by coral barriers and islands which divide the deep blue South Pacific Ocean from the placid inner reef waters. As Joseph Banks noted in 1770, "(the Reef) is a wall of coral rock, rising almost perpendicularly out of the unfathomable ocean...The large waves of the vast ocean meeting with so sudden a resistance make here a most terrible surf, breaking mountains high."

Behind the barrier's protection is a marine paradise of brilliant colour and form; here are 4,000 kinds of molluscs, thousands of other invertebrates and at least 1,500 species of fish. These, plus seabirds, marine mammals, reptiles - all can be seen in the wonderful world of Australia's Great Barrier Reef.

Beaked Coral Fish and hard coral

ABOVE RIGHT: GORGONIAN CORAL FAN.
CENTRE RIGHT: GREEN ISLAND, OFF CAIRNS.
RIGHT: GREEN TURTLE IS COMMON ON THE REEF.
OPPOSITE: TOP LEFT AND CLOCKWISE: TREVALLY; MANTA RAY; HORNED CORALFISH; MAKING BARRIER REEF DISCOVERIES; RECORDING HISTORY AT LADY ELLIOT ISLAND; OFF THE EDGE; UNDERWATER PHOTOGRAPHY.

53

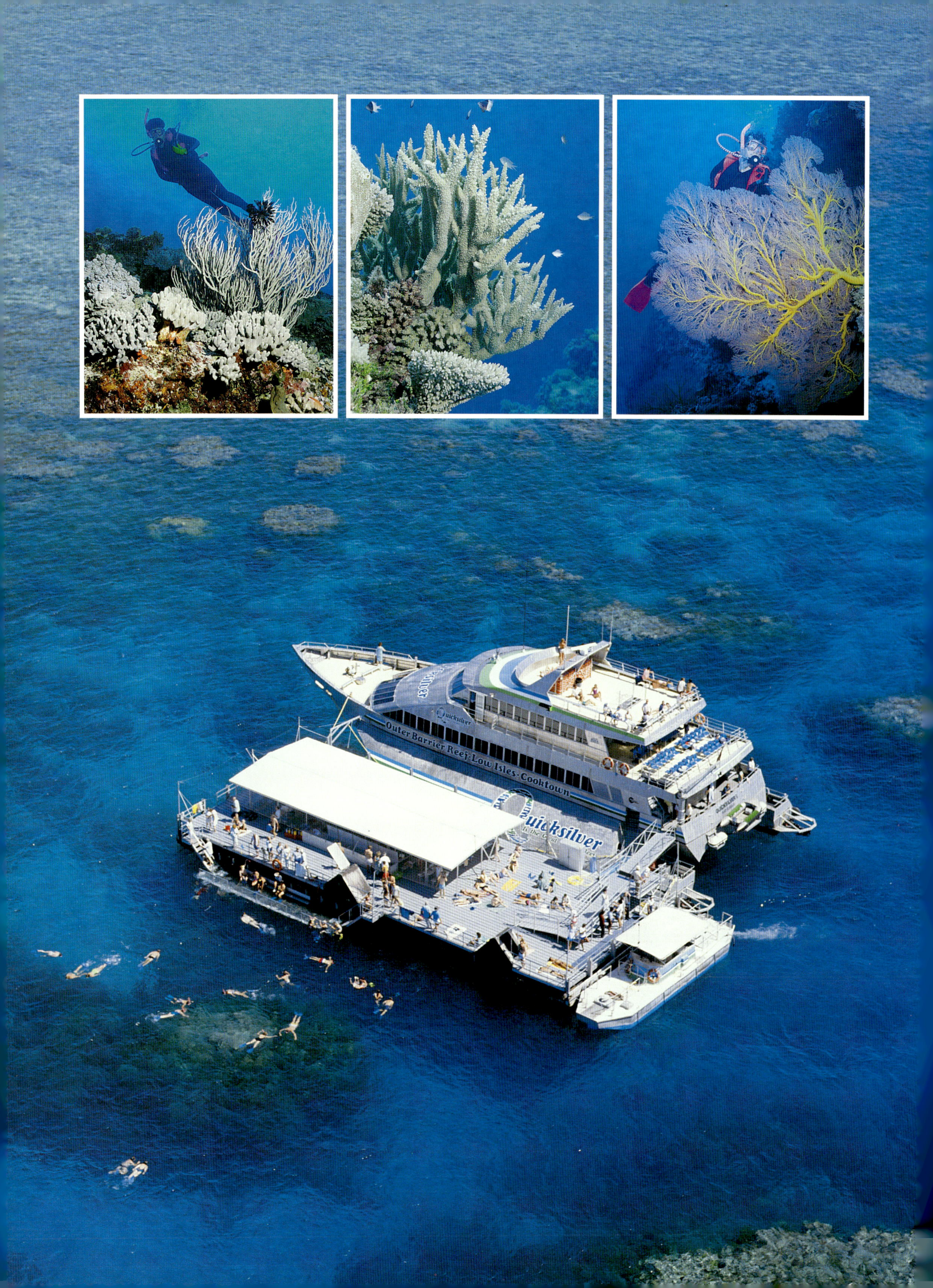
Outer Barrier Reef · Low Isles · Cooktown

TOP LEFT AND RIGHT: MILMAN ISLAND; HERON ISLAND.
CENTRE LEFT AND RIGHT: THE LOW ISLES; FITZROY ISLAND.
ABOVE LEFT TO RIGHT: DAMSELFISH; PINK ANEMONE FISH; EMPEROR ANGELFISH.
OPPOSITE: DIVE BOATS CARRY EAGER UNDERWATER EXPLORERS TO VIEW THE WONDERS OF THE REEF.

BRISBANE, THE GOLD AND SUNSHINE COASTS

"Beautiful one day, glorious the next!" is the traditional description of the southern coastline of Queensland on which stands the State capital, Brisbane. Australia's third largest city began in 1824, when convicts and soldiers landed at Redcliffe. Much has changed since those early days, fuelled by the wealth of southeast Queensland's pastureland, minerals, timber and other natural resources. Today, the economy of the State continues buoyant and Brisbane is a dynamic city, a growth centre of industry and commerce.

South of Brisbane lies the Gold Coast, 35 kilometres of superb Pacific beaches and mini-cities which offer a variety of lifestyles. Inland are ranges green with rainforest and full of fascinating wildlife.

North of Brisbane, the Sunshine Coast offers sun, surf and sailing, access to the Great Sandy wilderness region and a hinterland of mountains, rainforests and fertile river valleys.

TOP LEFT AND CLOCKWISE: SOUTH BANK, BESIDE THE BRISBANE RIVER; RIVERSIDE MARKETS AND THE *KOOKABURRA QUEEN* PADDLEWHEELER.; A VIEW OVER THE RIVERSIDE MARKETS TO SOME OF BRISBANE'S SHINING TOWERS; KODAK BEACH, SOUTH BANK.
OPPOSITE: NIGHT FALLS ON THE BRISBANE RIVER, RIVERSIDE CENTRE AND BRISBANE CITY.

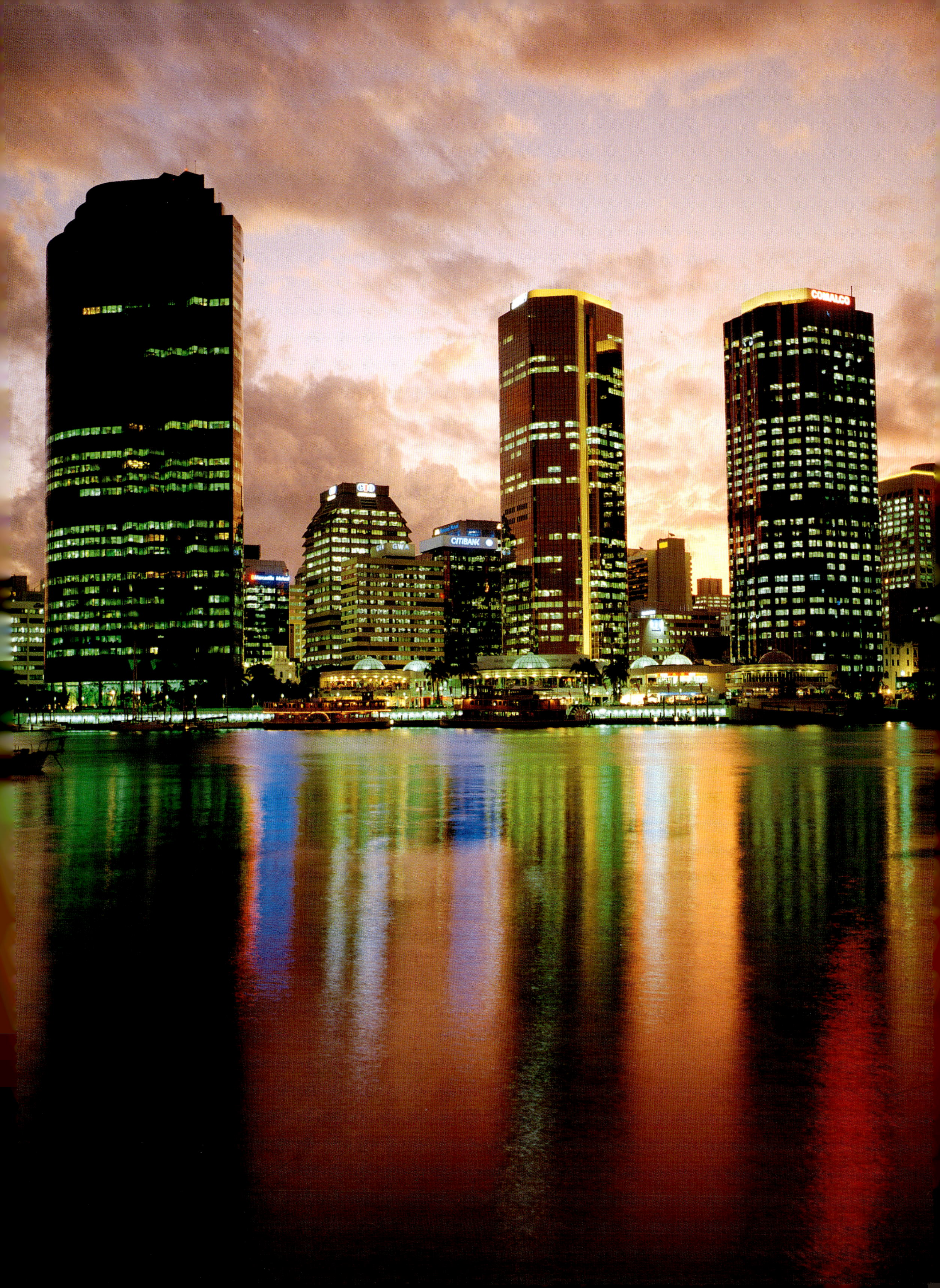
COMALCO
CITIBANK

TOP LEFT AND CLOCKWISE: CURRUMBIN SANCTUARY ON THE GOLD COAST; BUSKING IN QUEEN STREET MALL, BRISBANE; FEEDING THE LORIKEETS AT CURRUMBIN; THE BIG PINEAPPLE AT WOOMBYE, NEAR THE SUNSHINE COAST; A TRADITIONAL WOODEN QUEENSLAND HOME; FISHING IS A POPULAR QUEENSLAND COASTAL PASTIME; SURFING AT THE GOLD COAST; CHALAHN FALLS, LAMINGTON NATIONAL PARK; SUNSET OVER THE GLASSHOUSE MOUNTAINS.

TOP: SANCTUARY COVE, WHERE THE LIFESTYLE INCLUDES SAILING AND POWERBOATING.
CENTRE: SEA, SAND AND SUNSHINE ARE THE HALLMARKS OF THE GOLD AND SUNSHINE COASTS.
ABOVE: SURFERS PARADISE STANDS BETWEEN THE PACIFIC OCEAN AND GREEN MOUNTAIN RANGES.

THE TROPICAL QUEENSLAND COAST

Cairns is the tourist capital for North Queensland. It is a beautiful city, built on a narrow, fertile coastal plain between rainforest-covered mountains and the tropical sea. From Cairns, you can visit the Atherton Tableland, with its ancient forests, magnificent lakes and waterfalls.

North of Cairns, the Captain Cook Highway hugs the coast to Mossman and Port Douglas. Follow the coast far enough and you will reach Cape Tribulation, where, in June 1770, Captain James Cook's ship *Endeavour* was impaled on a coral reef. You can travel south of Cairns to Queensland's highest mountain, Bartle Frere, and further still, through sugarcane growing country, to the busy town of Rockhampton, or to Townsville, whose Common is a magnet for birdwatchers.

Coastal North Queensland offers a wide variety of experiences, from bareboating in the Whitsundays to fishing on the Great Barrier Reef, exploring primeval rainforests, or just relaxing under the palm trees on some remote beach, watching fluffy white clouds drift across an azure sky.

TOP LEFT AND CLOCKWISE: CAPE YORK, THE NORTHERNMOST POINT OF AUSTRALIA; CAIRNS BY NIGHT; SAILING IN THE WHITSUNDAYS; TOWNSVILLE, WITH CASTLE ROCK IN THE BACKGROUND; SUGARCANE IS GROWN ON THE FERTILE COASTAL PLAIN; CAIRNS ESPLANADE AND WATERFRONT DEVELOPMENT; CAIRNS; WATERBIRDS ON TOWNSVILLE COMMON; NORTH QUEENSLAND IS FOR MANY A TROPICAL DREAMLAND.
OPPOSITE: MAIN PICTURE: CAIRNS STANDS BETWEEN RAINFOREST AND REEF.
OPPOSITE: INSET LEFT AND RIGHT: ULYSSES BUTTERFLY; COOKTOWN ORCHID.

QUEENSLAND'S NORTHERN TROPICAL RAINFOREST MAGIC.
ABOVE LEFT AND CLOCKWISE: CUSCUS; STRIPED POSSUM, CRIMSON ROSELLA;
GREEN IS THE COLOUR OF RAINFOREST; ENJOYING RAINFOREST; SOUTHERN CASSOWARY.
OPPOSITE: TROPICAL RAINFOREST RUNS DOWN TO THE SEA NEAR CAPE TRIBULATION.

Map of Australia

Seas and Oceans:
- TIMOR SEA
- TORRES STRAIT
- GULF OF CARPENTARIA
- CORAL SEA
- INDIAN OCEAN
- PACIFIC OCEAN
- SOUTHERN OCEAN
- GREAT AUSTRALIAN BIGHT
- TASMAN SEA
- BASS STRAIT

States and Territories:
- NORTHERN TERRITORY
- QUEENSLAND
- WESTERN AUSTRALIA
- SOUTH AUSTRALIA
- NEW SOUTH WALES
- VICTORIA
- TASMANIA
- A.C.T.

Regions and Features:
- Bathurst Island
- Melville Island
- Cape York
- Arnhem Land
- Cape York Peninsula
- Great Barrier Reef
- Kimberley Division
- Great Sandy Desert
- Pilbara
- North West Cape
- MacDonnell Ranges
- Simpson Desert
- Great Victoria Desert
- Goldfields
- Eyre Peninsula
- Murray River
- Great Dividing Range
- Tropic of Capricorn
- SHARK BAY
- Dirk Hartog Is
- Kangaroo Is
- Rottnest Is
- Fraser Is
- Cape Naturaliste
- Cape Leeuwin
- Cape Arid
- Cape Byron
- Southwest Cape

Cities and Towns:
- DARWIN
- Wyndham
- Derby
- Broome
- Halls Creek
- Katherine
- Borroloola
- Burketown
- Cooktown
- Cairns
- Townsville
- Port Hedland
- Marble Bar
- Exmouth
- Tennant Creek
- Mount Isa
- Winton
- Longreach
- Rockhampton
- Alice Springs
- Birdsville
- Carnarvon
- Charleville
- Bundaberg
- Toowoomba
- BRISBANE
- Sunshine Coast
- Gold Coast
- Geraldton
- Kalgoorlie
- PERTH
- Fremantle
- Esperance
- Bunbury
- Albany
- Port Augusta
- Whyalla
- Port Pirie
- Port Lincoln
- ADELAIDE
- Victor Harbor
- Bourke
- Cobar
- Broken Hill
- Wentworth
- Swan Hill
- Echuca
- Albury
- Ballarat
- Geelong
- MELBOURNE
- Warrnambool
- Terrigal
- SYDNEY
- CANBERRA
- Burnie
- Launceston
- Richmond
- HOBART